Chinese FDI in the EU and the US

Tim Wenniges • Walter Lohman
Editors

Chinese FDI in the EU and the US

Simple Rules for Turbulent Times

palgrave
macmillan

Editors
Tim Wenniges
SUEDWESTMETALL – Employers' Association of the Metal and Electrical Industry of Baden-Wuerttemberg
Stuttgart, Germany

Walter Lohman
The Heritage Foundation
Washington, DC, USA

ISBN 978-981-13-6070-1   ISBN 978-981-13-6071-8 (eBook)
https://doi.org/10.1007/978-981-13-6071-8

Library of Congress Control Number: 2019932977

This Palgrave Macmillan imprint is published by the registered company Springer Nature Singapore Pte Ltd.
The registered company address is: 152 Beach Road, #21-01/04 Gateway East, Singapore 189721, Singapore

Preface

In a 2012 *Harvard Business Review* article previewing their subsequent book, *Simple Rules: How to Survive in a Complex World*, management gurus Donald Sull and Kathleen M. Eisenhardt suggest a set of rules to bridge between a company's strategy and its execution. Although written with business management in mind, it is a concept with important application to international economic interaction—in particular, the West's relationship with China.

We will let the reader deduce from the readings that follow what these rules should entail. For our part, we would like to lay out what we think the strategic objectives of Europe-US economic engagement with China should be and point the reader to where he might find the rules to govern them.

As we see it, there are four objectives that should guide the relationship:

1. **Maximize China's positive contributions to our own national economies, and by extension, the global economy**. China is simply too big an economy today, too deeply embedded in the economic future of its neighbors and the world to ignore or to treat it as a Cold War–type adversary. Its reform and rapid development since 1978 is a good thing for the world. It is in the interest of all concerned that it continues to grow in prosperity.
2. **Prioritize the needs of global value chains and consumers**. From investment to sale, the objective of governments ought to be—to the greatest extent possible and within the bounds of prudent

regulation—to enable global commerce. Whether it is American or European investment in China, or Chinese investment in the West, decisions should be based on considerations of efficiency and effectiveness, with limited government interference.

3. **Account for differences in the Chinese and Western governance models**. The US and Europe have differences in the way their governments interact with the private sector. The differences in their approaches, however, pale in comparison to the differences they each have with Chinese state-led capitalism. This raises important issues of fairness and reciprocity.
4. **Guard against security threats**. Because the state is so heavily involved in the investment decisions of both Chinese private and state-owned companies, there is a natural and justified suspicion of their motives. This is compounded by a foreign policy that appears intent on establishing dominance in the Indo-Pacific and deference to Chinese political/security interests. It is not always clear whether investment decisions are being made for the benefit of the companies' bottom line or for these broader political/security objectives of the Chinese state. In order to come to the point one has to be precise: Not every investment decision might be politically motivated, but there is no bigger investment without the political backing by the Communist Party of China (CPC).

In order to point the reader in the direction of the rules that can guide him toward these objectives, we cite below Sull and Eisenhardt's "Rules for Developing Simple Rules" and indicate what each might mean for Europe-US engagement with China:

1. "**Identify a bottleneck that is both specific and strategic**." "Bottleneck" is a term especially applicable to business. It is a point in the production process that inhibits efficiency. But although it is a business term, it is not difficult to imagine the ways in which it might apply in this case. Consider the multitude of restrictions on foreign investment in China, inefficient intra-governmental processes there and corruption. Investment approval processes in the US, the European Union (EU) and EU member countries are some other possible targets.
2. "**Let data trump opinion**." This is a warning against allowing the heat of the moment or politics to skew an objective reading of the

environment. This is such vital advice. In a world awash in opinion, the data and true historical record often have a difficult time getting through. A very common example of this in the current case is the routine misstatement of China's record in the World Trade Organization (WTO). Yes, China presents the body unique and difficult issues, and yes, its record of compliance with WTO's terms of accession is mixed. It has, however, often been successfully challenged at the WTO and complied with the body's findings. Issues surrounding intellectual property rights in China is another area of heated commentary that generates little light. China coerces multinational companies to relinquish intellectual property. There is no question about this. Nevertheless, it is necessary to put some finer points on the charge. What have been the circumstances of the coercion? To what extent have companies facilitated their own victimization in pursuit of market share?

3. "**Users make the rules**." In the context of China-Western economic relations, this strikes us as a plea to prioritize the views of the businesses and consumers. The businesses interacting with Chinese authorities have no motive except return on investment and the long-term health of their enterprises. Their concerns about access to the Chinese market must be front and center. Do these businesses welcome Chinese investment in their home markets? Why or why not? As long as neither of these expressions seek unfair advantage, they represent the most authoritative view of the respective investment climates. Similar logic applies to consumers and their access to affordable, quality choices. None of these decisions are best left to government.
4. "**The rules should be concrete**." Politics may be a destructive force in developing rules. Broad characterization of Chinese strategy and tactics can cloud the very specific issue that must be addressed. For instance, alarm that the Chinese are "stealing our jobs," "ripping us off" or "robbing us of our crown jewels" may lead to a rule to prevent such from occurring. Yet, such a rule says nothing about specifically how this is happening, or in fact, whether it is happening at all. As a result, it could lead to a rule based on false premises that unnecessarily inhibit efficiency and effectiveness. Security concerns, in particular, must be very concrete. Without a concrete definition of national security threat, almost any parochial concern can qualify for government protection.

5. **"The rules should evolve**." Circumstances change. The West largely understands free market reform in China to have regressed. That may change, however. Reform may return, either broadly or in particular sectors. We should be open to the prospect of this. As importantly, we have to be cognizant of how the rules we develop work in practice and adjust as necessary in order to achieve our stated objectives. If the Chinese, for example, exploit specific vulnerabilities in our investment screening processes, those processes must be tightened. By the same token, if they proved to restrict harmless investment, they must also be adjusted.

The objectives of Europe-US economic engagement with China do not pull in a single direct. In some ways, they are contradictory, for example, security versus economic freedom. Similarly, the "rules to develop simple rules" will not lead to conclusions that are not without contradiction. This is by design. We do indeed live in a "complex world." Only by being conscious of the various aims of public policy, even when they work against one another, can officials develop frameworks with the prospect of serving them all.

With these considerations in mind, we invite the reader to think about the rules implied in the following pages. What specific action can be taken that both facilitates prosperity-generating economic interaction and guards against security threats? What measures can promote reciprocity in the treatment of international business without harming the benefits of economic freedom? How do we deal with a China that has such a clearly different governance model than our own? These are just small samples of the questions the following essays should provoke. The answers we leave to you.

Some might wonder about the selection of authors. In fact we have talked to several decision makers from politics, institutions, business and labor unions—in the US, the EU and China. Many have been keen to contribute, but had (mainly internal) reasons not to. This makes us even more proud to present a list of such distinguished persons who were able to write on this issue. It is our hope that we will be able to follow up with this piece in a version with Chinese officials. So far this book should serve as a starting point for a more elaborated debate on how to deal with China aside the glorification and demonization of the Chinese model.

Stuttgart, Germany — Tim Wenniges
Washington, DC — Walter Lohman

Contents

Notes on Contributors

Diego Andreis is the Managing Director of Fluid-o-Tech Srl, a family business with more than 70 years of experience in the engineering and manufacturing of positive displacement pumps and fluidics systems for the automotive, medical, food service and industrial field. In 2015 he became president of the Assolombarda Mechatronics Companies Group and vice president of Federmeccanica, in charge of relations with multinationals and large enterprises in Europe. In September 2016 he was appointed president of the European employers' organization Ceemet, representing 200,000 companies. He is also a member of Aspen Institute Italia.

Edwin Feulner the retired president of the Heritage Foundation and a long-time commentator on and participant in international trade issues. Two of his earliest publications are *Trading with Communists* (with Samuel F. Clabaugh, 1968) and *Congress and the New International Economic Order* (1976).

Thorsten Frei is Member of the German Parliament since 2013, vice-chairman of CDU/CSU parliamentary group in charge of interior and judicial affairs since 2018 and vice-chairman of the Christian Democratic Union (CDU) in the state of Baden-Württemberg. Before he served as Mayor of Donaueschingen, he held several positions in the CDU in Germany. He has been member of the Foreign Committee of the German Parliament and was part of the Party dialogue between the CDU and the Communist Party of China.

Roland Freudenstein is the policy director of the Wilfried Martens Centre for European Studies. After a two-year voluntary military service, he studied political science, economics, Japan studies and international relations in Bonn and Los Angeles. He became a member of the foreign and security planning staff of the European Commission in Brussels in the 1990s. Subsequently, he became the director of the Warsaw office of the Konrad Adenauer Foundation and later held a leading function in the Foundation's central office in Berlin. He has contributed to debates and written articles extensively on European integration, international security, German-Polish relations, global democracy support and about Russia and Eastern Europe.

Jürgen M. Geißinger is a German technology business executive and is best known for his 15-year role as the Chief Executive of Schaeffler AG. In addition to this, he was the CEO of the windturbine manufacturer Senvion S.A. He is an entrepreneur and investor and is also the chairman of the International Commission of the Economic Council (Wirtschaftsrat der CDU e. V.) in Germany.

Peter Goettler is President and CEO of the Cato Institute in Washington, DC. Before joining Cato, Goettler was Head of Investment Banking and Debt Capital Markets-Americas, Head of Global Leveraged Finance, and Head of Global Loans at Barclays Capital. He concurrently served as CEO of Latin America for Barclays plc.

Daniel Ikenson is Director of the Herbert A. Stiefel Center for Trade Policy Studies at the Cato Institute in Washington, DC. In that capacity, Ikenson coordinates and conducts research on all manner of international trade and investment policy. Since joining Cato in 2000, Ikenson has authored or coauthored dozens of papers, book chapters, and a book on various aspects of US trade policy, including US-China economic relations, bilateral and multilateral trade agreements and institutions, the trade remedy laws, foreign direct investment and the politics of trade.

Jyrki Katainen is a Finnish politician and the European Commission Vice President for Jobs, Growth, Investment and Competitiveness, in office since 2014. Katainen was previously Prime Minister of Finland from 2011 to 2014 and chairman of the National Coalition Party from 2004 to 2014. He was succeeded by Alexander Stubb as chairman of Finland's National Coalition Party. After stepping down as prime minister, Katainen was elected as the European Commission Vice President in July 2014.

Dieter Kempf is currently President of the Federation of German Industries, BDI. After studying business administration from 1973 to 1978 in Munich, he worked at Arthur & Young (now Ernst & Young) from 1978 to 1991, becoming a partner in 1989. He then joined Datev in Nuremberg in 1991 as a board member, responsible for product and software development. From 1992 onward, he served as deputy chairman of the board. In 1996, he became chairman, a position he held until March 2016. During Kempf's time at Datev, the company grew to one of Europe's largest IT service providers. From 2011 to 2015, Kempf served as president of BDI's member association, Bitkom (Federal Association for Information Technology, Telecommunications and New Media). During this time, he was also vice president of the BDI. Kempf was unanimously elected president of BDI as of January 2017. In addition, he serves on various supervisory boards and advisory boards. He was made honorary professor of Friedrich-Alexander University of Erlangen-Nürnberg in 2005.

Changfeng Tu assists Chinese clients with their merger and acquisition transactions and other investments in Germany and Europe, and also advises German and European clients on investments in China. Beyond advising on the legal aspects of a transaction, Tu provides intercultural understanding in order to bring transactions to a successful close. He studied law at Bonn University, where he received his PhD in 2006. Tu also passed the First and the Second German State Examination in Law and was admitted to the German bar in 2006. After working in the Duesseldorf office of Hengeler Mueller, he moved to Shanghai in 2014, where he now heads the firm's local office.

Britta Vasters is the head of the international department at the Economic Council (Wirtschaftsrat der CDU e. V.) in Germany. She started as a research fellow at the European Parliament and German Bundestag and worked for the German Chamber of Commerce in Shanghai and the Association of German Chambers of Commerce and Industry in Berlin. In cooperation with the Chinese embassy she established the German-Chinese Economic Dialogue in Berlin, a platform for German and Chinese decision-makers. She has published various articles about the German-Chinese economic relations, international markets and free trade agreements for instance at the "Magazin für Soziale Marktwirtschaft." She is fluent in Mandarin.

Lutz-Christian Wolff is the Dean of the Graduate School and Wei Lun Professor of Law at, The Chinese University of Hong Kong. He specializes in International and Chinese Business Law, Comparative Law and Private International Law. He has studied, worked and conducted research in a number of jurisdictions, including mainland China, Taiwan, and the US. He is admitted to practice in England & Wales and in Germany. He is frequently invited to work with multinational companies on investment projects in the Greater China region.

Joachim Wuermeling is member of the executive board of the Deutsche Bundesbank, currently responsible for the Directorates of General Banking and Financial Supervision, Information Technology and Risk Control. Before that, he served as State Secretary at the Federal Ministry for Economics and Technology, where he was responsible for coordinating European policy matters. Wuermeling is member of the ECB Supervisory Board, the Basel Committee on Banking Supervision (BCBS) and the German Financial Stability Committee.

Jörg Wuttke has been head of a major European multinational company since 1997. From 2001 to 2004 Wuttke was the chairman of the German Chamber of Commerce in China. From 2007 to 2010, and 2014 to 2017, he was the president of the European Union Chamber of Commerce in China. Wuttke is member of the advisory board of Germany's foremost think tank on China, Mercator Institute for China Studies (MERICS), in Berlin. From 2013 to 2016, and again since 2019, he is vice chairman of the CPCIF International Cooperation Committee, a group representing multinational companies in China's chemical association. Wuttke holds a BA in Business Administration and Economics from Mannheim and studied Chinese in Shanghai in 1982 and in Taipei from 1984 to 1985.

CHAPTER 1

Chinese Outbound Investments

Changfeng Tu

Starting Point: Prior to the Global Financial Crisis

In the beginning of the twenty-first century, China was one of the world's major recipients of foreign investment, while its role as an outbound investor was still insignificant. In 1999, the Chinese government issued a new going-out policy to encourage Chinese companies to invest overseas. Since the mid-2000s Chinese outbound non-financial foreign direct investment (FDI) experienced a continuous, but unremarkable increase. After the global financial crisis of 2008, however, growth rates started to accelerate notably—the global financial crisis also changed the landscape of the Chinese overseas FDI.

In the first years of the new millennium, the international merger and acquisition (M&A) market prospered, driven and accomplished by the globalization process and other cross-border activities, such as the integration of the global financial markets. Thanks to the highly liquid capital

Ms Gesche Heidorn, Ms Li Wang and Dr. Deniz Tschammler provided great support for the preparation of this chapter.

C. Tu (✉)
Partner of Hengeler Mueller, Shanghai, China
e-mail: changfeng.tu@hengeler.com

T. Wenniges, W. Lohman (eds.), *Chinese FDI in the EU and the US*,
https://doi.org/10.1007/978-981-13-6071-8_1

market, financial investors were able to use high leverage to reach high return. The sub-prime crisis followed by the global financial crisis was the turning point, which completely changed the market. The economy floated down and banks and the capital market were not able anymore to provide favorable financing. Both strategic and financial investors were reluctant to invest. However, on the other hand, policy restrictions of the Chinese government on cross-board capital flows had ring-fenced China's financial system and protected it from direct disruption by the financial crisis to certain extents, although the Chinese export suffered under the global recession caused by the financial crisis. In total, China was less exposed to the global financial crisis than other economies and not directly affected by the sub-prime mortgage problem.[1]

As global direct investment flows dropped in the aftermath of the financial crisis, China started to play an increasing role as providers of overseas FDI.

Going Out During and After the Financial Crisis

In the years after 2008, China became more and more influential as an overseas investor. Although most transactions during the financial crisis were organized as auctions, the Chinese investors were in many cases one of the few bidders who were able to submit competitive offers. On the other hand, Chinese companies were faced with a slowing down of the domestic economy, increasing competition in the domestic market and devaluation pressure on the Chinese currency. Cross-border M&A presents a possibility to increase market share abroad, to realize further growths as well as to access brands and technology, which first and foremost strengthened the competitive ability of the Chinese investors in the Chinese domestic market. In addition, in certain industrial sectors, outbound investments of Chinese A-share listed companies were also driven by the high equity valuation in the Chinese equity capital market. Many of the Chinese financial investors, for example, private equity funds or investment funds, also used the Chinese equity capital market as an exit for their cross-border M&A transactions.

[1] *See also* Daniel C.K. Chow, *China's Response to the Global Financial Crisis: Implications for U.S.—China Economic Relations*, 1 Global Bus. L. Rev. 47 (2010), p. 63.

Most of the Chinese investors started as beginners in the cross-border M&A business. However, they quickly developed their skills in the field and, years later, were in many cases able to successfully compete with their international competitors in competitive auction processes. The substantial increase in the number and complexity of corporate transactions caused a shift in China's global investment position.

Already in 2011, China had become the world's sixth largest source of FDI[2] and, in the following years, continued to manifest its position as one of the top direct investor nations globally. In 2014, China's overseas investments rose by 14.1% to $102.9 billion, while inbound FDI only rose by 1.7%.[3] China's share as a foreign investor in Europe increased considerably from 0.3% in 1995 to 2% in 2015.[4] Investments also saw a shift in sector composition, from natural resources in developing countries to technology, brands, real estates and other assets in high-income economies.[5] State-owned enterprises accounted for a majority of China's cross-border investments, with the share increasing from 62% in 2014 to 70% in 2015.[6]

During the global financial crisis, Chinese investments were welcome also in the US and European countries. In some cases, Chinese investors used their network and distribution channel in their Chinese home market to help their acquired foreign subsidiaries to gain more market access and market share in China, which helped the foreign subsidiaries overcome the financial crisis and the recession. The leverage on such potential synergy in China is often also the economic basis for a higher premium offered by Chinese bidders in global M&A auctions. The valuation gap between the

[2] Kefei You, *What drives China's outward FDI? A regional analysis*, BOFIT Discussion Papers 16 (2015), p. 5.

[3] Lihuan Zhou/Denise Leung, *China's Overseas Investments, Explained in 10 Graphics* (January 28, 2015), https://www.wri.org/blog/2015/01/china%E2%80%99s-overseas-investments-explained-10-graphics (accessed September 21, 2018).

[4] European Commission, *Proposal for a Regulation of the European Parliament and of the Council establishing a framework for screening of foreign direct investments into the European Union*, SWD(2017) 297 final, https://ec.europa.eu/transparency/regdoc/rep/1/2017/EN/COM-2017-487-F1-EN-MAIN-PART-1.PDF (accessed February 25, 2019), p. 3.

[5] Thilo Hanemann/Mikko Huotari, *Preparing for a new era of Chinese Capital. Chinese FDI in Europe and Germany*, Merics Paper on China, June 2015, https://www.merics.org/sites/default/files/2018-07/COFDI_2015_EN_web.pdf (accessed September 21, 2018), p. 5.

[6] Thilo Hanemann/Mikko Huotari, *A New Record Year for Chinese Outbound Investment in Europe*, Merics Paper on China, February 2016, https://www.merics.org/sites/default/files/2018-07/COFDI_2016_web.pdf (accessed September 21, 2018), p. 5.

international equity market and the Chinese equity capital markets also helped Chinese bidders to offer competitive purchase prices.

On the other hand, these new Chinese investments in the Western receiving countries were unprecedented in history and have been under close observation of the recipient countries and often associated with different concerns and worries.

For industrial countries there has been the question, ever since the beginning of the recent development of Chinese overseas FDI, whether their industry would sell out its technology to China, which builds the basis for the prosperity and wealth of society, and thereby lose its technological advantage toward China.[7] Such concerns and worries have also been, to certain extent, fueled by ambitious Chinese domestic industry policies, such as the so-called *Made in China 2025* initiative.

Another concern of the local press of the Western receiving countries is that the Chinese takeover of the companies would lead to loss of jobs and deterioration of employer-labor relations. Apart from distressed transactions, which are often followed by a restructuring process, such concerns and worries have rarely been confirmed in the praxis.[8]

Slowing Down After the OFDI Boom in 2016

In 2016, China saw its strongest annual growth of overseas FDI. According to China's Ministry of Commerce (MOFCOM), Chinese overseas FDI surged by 44.1% to a record value of USD 170.11 billion.[9] In Europe—one of the key destinations—Chinese investments increased by 77%,[10] with Germany being the largest European recipient.[11]

In 2017, however, the value of Chinese overseas FDI fell sharply by 29.4% to USD 120.1 billion, marking the first drop after more than one

[7] An example hereof is the reaction of the German society and government regarding the takeover of Kuka by Media in 2016.

[8] More details also in: Wolfgang Müller, *Chinesische Investoren und Auswirkungen auf Arbeitsbeziehungen und Mitbestimmung*, Hans-Böckler-Stiftung, https://www.boeckler.de/pdf/p_mbf_report_2017_36_ci_mueller.pdf (accessed February 25, 2019).

[9] The State Council, *China's ODI up 44.1% in 2016*, http://english.gov.cn/archive/statistics/2017/01/16/content_281475543375328.htm (accessed September 5, 2018).

[10] Thilo Hanemann/Mikko Huotari, *Record Flows and Growing Imbalances*, Merics Paper on China, January 2017, https://www.merics.org/en/node/6721 (accessed February 25, 2019), pp. 4–5, with an overview of the biggest transactions in 2016.

[11] In 2016, Chinese FDI flows into Germany were greater than German FDI flows into China; Hanemann/Huotari, *Record Flows and Growing Imbalances*, p. 8.

decade of continuous growth.[12] The first half of 2018 deepened geographic discrepancies in Chinese overseas FDI activity. While investment in Europe slowly recovered in the first six months of 2018, investment in the US experienced a continuous decline.[13]

As will be discussed below, the decline is both attributable to Beijing's tightening on regulatory control over capital outflow and enhanced screening mechanisms of Western recipient countries.[14] In addition, the threatening trade war between the US and China could also add further headwind for Chinese overseas FDI.

The Numbers: Development of Chinese Overseas FDI in 2017 and 2018

Europe saw a comparatively moderate drop in 2017, amounting only to 17%,[15] while in the US, the volume of completed transactions declined sharply by 35%.[16] In terms of new activity in the US, there was even a drop of 90% compared to the record year of 2016.[17] The decline in the US was strongest in entertainment, consumer products, services and real estate as well as in hospitality.[18]

Already in the second half of 2017, Chinese investment momentum rebounded in Europe.[19] Meanwhile, the US saw a further decline. In the

[12] Zhou Xin, *China Focus: China 2017 FDI rises to record high, ODI falls*, XinhuaNet, http://www.xinhuanet.com/english/2018-01/16/c_136900334.htm (accessed September 5, 2018).

[13] However, the numbers are still remarkably higher than before the peak in 2016. According to data compiled by Thomson Reuters, ChinaVenture, AVCJ public news and PwC analysis, numbers of the total deal values in the first half of 2018 are still about a third higher than the levels seen before 2016; see PwC, *PwC M&A 2018 Mid-Year Review and Outlook*, https://www.pwccn.com/en/deals/publications/ma-2018-mid-year-review-and-outlook.pdf (accessed September 21, 2018), p. 29.

[14] Thilo Hanemann/Mikko Huotari, *EU-China FDI: Working towards Reciprocity in investment relations*, Merics Papers on China, May 2018, https://www.merics.org/sites/default/files/2018-08/180723_MERICS-COFDI-Update_final.pdf (accessed September 5, 2018), p. 29.

[15] Hanemann/Huotari, *EU-China FDI: Working towards Reciprocity in investment relations*, p. 30.

[16] Thilo Hanemann/Daniel Rosen, *Chinese FDI in the US in 2017: A Double Policy Punch*, Rhodium Group, https://rhg.com/research/chinese-fdi-in-the-us-in-2017-a-double-policy-punch/ (accessed February 25, 2019).

[17] Ibid.

[18] Ibid.

[19] Hanemann/Huotari, *EU-China FDI: Working towards Reciprocity in investment relations*, p. 29.

first half of 2018, newly announced Chinese M&A transactions only amounted to USD 2.5 billion—the lowest level seen in a decade—compared to a value of USD 20 billion in Europe.[20] Sweden was the largest European destination in 2018 (USD 3.6 billion), followed by the UK (USD 1.6 billion), Germany (USD 1.5 billion) and France (USD 1.4 billion).[21]

Both Europe and North America also experienced a shift in industry composition of overseas FDI flows. In Europe, the biggest sectors for Chinese FDI in 2017 were agriculture and food (56%), transport and infrastructure (22%), and information and communication technology (7%) along with real estate and hospitality (4%).[22] In the first half of 2018, transport and infrastructure (31%), health and biotech (19%) and consumer products and services (11%) became the top sectors.[23]

In North America, the biggest sectors in 2017 were real estate and hospitality (38%) as well as transport and infrastructure (35%). In the first half of 2018, the biggest sector was health care and biotech (54%).[24]

The Chinese Perspective

Restricting Outflows

By end of 2016, China's foreign currency reserves dropped from USD 4 trillion to 3 trillion within less than two years. Responding to the growing capital outflows, and to prevent a further drain on China's foreign currency reserves and reduce the pressure on the Chinese currency, PBOC, the Chinese central bank and other government agencies strengthened the overseas FDI reviews.

In August 2017, the National Development and Reform Commission (NDRC) introduced a codified regulatory pathway for OFDI transaction approval. This new OFDI management system distinguishes between

[20] Baker McKenzie, *Chinese Investing Nine Times More in Europe Than North America as Policies Force Divergence* (July 16, 2018), https://www.bakermckenzie.com/en/newsroom/2018/07/chinese-fdi-h1-2018 (accessed February 25, 2019).

[21] Natasha Turak, *China is investing 9 times more into Europe than into North America, report reveals* (July 17, 2018), CNBC, (July 17, 2018), https://www.cnbc.com/2018/07/17/china-is-investing-9-times-more-into-europe-than-into-north-america.html (accessed September 5, 2018).

[22] Baker McKenzie, *New policies take effect. Beijing has restricted investment in the real estate, hospitality, entertainment and financial sectors*, https://www.bakermckenzie.com/en/insight/publications/2018/08/china-fdi (accessed September 5, 2018).

[23] Ibid.

[24] Ibid.

different types of encouraged, restricted and prohibited investments.[25] The controls mainly target private enterprises. Consequently, while both private and state-owned enterprises (SOEs) have seen a slide in activity, the negative effect on private companies was stronger.[26]

Strengthening BRI Investment

Even while generally restricting capital outflow, China continues to encourage overseas FDI to countries involved in the Belt and Road Initiative (BRI): "[T]he Belt and Road Initiative aims to promote the connectivity of Asian, European and African continents and their adjacent seas, establish and strengthen partnerships among the countries along the Belt and Road, set up all-dimensional, multitiered and composite connectivity networks, and realize diversified, independent, balanced and sustainable development in these countries".[27]

This initiative consists primarily of the Silk Road Economic Belt, linking China to Central and South Asia and onward to Europe, and the New Maritime Silk Road, linking China to the nations of Southeast Asia, the Gulf countries, and North Africa and on to Europe.[28] The countries included account for half the world's population and a quarter of global GDP,[29] with its geographic scope of constantly expanding. In the five years

[25] Encouraged transactions include infrastructure projects that are part of the Belt and Road Initiatives, high-tech businesses, advanced manufacturing enterprises, overseas research and development, agriculture, energy resources and services sectors. Restricted industries include real estate, sports clubs, hotels, entertainment and the film industry, while overseas FDI into gambling or sex industries is prohibited; see Betty Huang/Le Xia, *China ODI from the Middle Kingdom: What's next after the big turnaround?*, BBVA Research, China Economic Watch, February 2018, https://www.bbvaresearch.com/wp-content/uploads/2018/02/201802_ChinaWatch_China-Outward-Investment_EDI.pdf (accessed September 5, 2018), p. 2.

[26] Huang/Xia, *China ODI from the Middle Kingdom: What's next after the big turnaround?*, pp. 6–7; PwC, *PwC M&A 2018 Mid-Year Review and Outlook*, p. 21.

[27] The State Council, Full text: *Action plan on the Belt and Road Initiative* (March 30, 2015), http://english.gov.cn/archive/publications/2015/03/30/content_281475080249035.htm (accessed September 21, 2018).

[28] The World Bank, *Belt and Road Initiative* (March 29, 2018), https://www.worldbank.org/en/topic/regional-integration/brief/belt-and-road-initiative (accessed September 21, 2018).

[29] Lily Kuo/Niko Kommenda, *What is China's Belt and Road Initiative?* (July 30, 2018), The Guardian, https://www.theguardian.com/cities/ng-interactive/2018/jul/30/what-china-belt-road-initiative-silk-road-explainer (accessed September 21, 2018).

after the launch of the project, China has invested more than USD 25 billion into BRI-related infrastructure projects.[30]

According to a press release by Xinhua, Chinese overseas FDI to BRI countries remained stable in 2017, amounting to USD 14.4 billion.[31] Because of the overall decline, the share of investment to BRI countries increased from 8.5% in 2016 to 12% in 2017 of total Chinese overseas FDI.[32]

Since the BRI initiative aims at increasing China's influence in its regional neighborhood and beyond, there are worries that the initiative may give China too much leverage on smaller and developing countries and too much geo-political power.

Receiving Countries' Perspective

Another factor for the decline in Chinese overseas FDI is an increasing regulatory pushback in receiving countries against Chinese takeovers. Many OECD (Organisation for Economic Co-operation and Development) economies have tightened or are in the process of reviewing their foreign investment security screening regimes, trying to strike a balance between the opportunities and the concerns associated with inbound investments.

The rising protectionist tendencies can be attributed to a changing attitude among policymakers toward China's economic strategies. There is an increased awareness of the potential security and economic risk associated with Chinese investment. In Europe, regulators both on the national and on the EU level expressed discomfort with the lack of reciprocity in trade relations and call for a level-playing field with regard to investment control.[33] It is the concern of the policymakers that the shift to

[30] Thomas S. Eder, *Mapping the Belt and Road initiative* (July 6, 2018), https://www.merics.org/en/bri-tracker/mapping-the-belt-and-road-initiative (accessed February 25, 2019).

[31] Zhou Xin, *China Focus: China 2017 FDI rises to record high, ODI falls*, XinhuaNet, http://www.xinhuanet.com/english/2018-01/16/c_136900334.htm (accessed September 5, 2018).

[32] Ibid.

[33] European Commission, *Communication from the Commission to the European Parliament, the European Council, the Council, the European Economic and Social Committee and the Committee of the Regions. Welcoming Foreign Direct Investment while Protecting Essential Interests*, COM (2017) 494 final, https://ec.europa.eu/transparency/regdoc/rep/1/2017/EN/COM-2017-494-F1-EN-MAIN-PART-1.PDF (accessed February 25, 2019), p. 7.

acquisitions in advanced technology has been promoted by Chinese policy plans, such as *Made in China 2025* initiative.[34] This development elicits fear that the transfer of core technology and know-how abroad will not only impact economic growth but also create potential long-term risks to national security. Such foreign investment security screening regimes toward Chinese investments generally enhanced the deal uncertainty for Chinese investors and make the Chinese investments more difficult and, in some cases, even impossible.

In case such foreign investment security screening regimes would target protection of its technological domination or goals other than the protection of national security, the questions for such administrative approach would be: Would the government know the value and importance of the targeted technology better than the company and the receiving country's shareholders themselves, and is such administrative approach the right and efficient way to achieve such goals?

Reforms in Germany

In July 2017 and December 2018, Germany substantially amended and strengthened its Foreign Trade and Payment Ordinance (New FTO), introducing stricter scrutiny in reviewing foreign direct investments into domestic companies.

The Federal Ministry for Economic Affairs and Energy has the competence to examine (and, together with the federal government, eventually prohibit or restrict) an acquisition through which an investor from outside the EU or European Free Trade Association will gain 25% or more of the voting rights in a German company. With effect from 29 December 2018, according to the New FTO, the threshold of 25% has been reduced to 10% regarding acquisitions of certain German companies which are considered particularly sensitive (in particular operators of critical infrastructures and companies in certain defense sectors).[35]

[34] European Commission, *Press Release, State of the Union 2017—Trade Package: European Commission proposes framework for screening of foreign direct investments* (September 14, 2017), http://europa.eu/rapid/press-release_IP-17-3183_en.htm (accessed February 25, 2019). For an overview on the sectoral composition of inward M&As from 1995 to 2016 in the EU, see European Commission, *Proposal for a Regulation of the European Parliament and of the Council establishing a framework for screening of foreign direct investments into the European Union*, SWD(2017) 297 final, p. 15.

[35] Federal Ministry for Economic Affairs, Press Release, Minister Zypries: "Fair competition and better protection in corporate acquisitions" (July 12, 2017), https://www.bmwi.

The New FTO now provides a non-exhaustive list specifying cases in which public order or security may in particular be threatened and which thus have to be notified to the ministry. According to the amended legislation, a threat to public order or security may exist in particular if the German target company operates a "critical infrastructure" or develops industry-specific software for such infrastructure.[36] The critical sectors include energy supply, information technology and communication, transport and haulage, health, water, nutrition, finance and insurance.

Also, the reform widened the scope of the so-called sector-specific examination, which concerns foreign investments into the German defense and encryption sector. When conducting this specific review, the German government applies a stricter standard of review and the buyer must notify the ministry and obtain clearance of the transaction before the deal can be closed.[37] The reform extended the catalogue for this examination to include companies which manufacture a variety of items specifically designed for military use.

Under the new rules, review deadlines are also extended significantly.[38] In case of an ex-officio examination, the expiry period only starts after the ministry gained knowledge of the transaction. In the absence of a notification, therefore, the ministry can now initiate an ex-post control of an investment for up to five years after closing. During the investigation proceedings all parties of the transaction may be under an obligation to provide information if requested by the ministry.

Even though the Ministry for Economic Affairs and Energy is expected to clear the vast majority of transactions, the new levels of scrutiny constitute a considerable transaction risk. Major obstacles include the high degree of exposure and uncertainty regarding the time frame, as excessive document request may cause substantial delays in the examination and clearance proceedings.

de/Redaktion/EN/Pressemitteilungen/2017/20170712-zypries-besserer-schutz-bei-firmenuebernahmen.html (accessed September 21, 2018).

[36] Wilmerhale, *German Government Amends German Foreign Trade and Payments Ordinance to Widen Control of Foreign Takeovers of Critical German Companies* (July 24, 2017), https://www.wilmerhale.com/en/insights/client-alerts/2017-07-24-german-government-amends-german-foreign-tradea-and-payments-ordinance-to-widen-control-of-foreign-takeovers-of-critical-german-companies (accessed September 21, 2018).

[37] Ibid.

[38] Federal Ministry for Economic Affairs, Press Release, Minister Zypries: "Fair competition and better protection in corporate acquisitions".

Proposed European Framework

Even though the EU emphasizes its continued openness to foreign direct investment as a source of growth and jobs, it has also started to send signals toward more scrutiny of potentially security-sensitive EU inbound investments.

In September 2017, on the initiative of Germany, France and Italy, the European Commission announced the proposal for a regulation establishing a framework for the screening of foreign direct investments into the EU. The proposed regulation is not designed to introduce a centralized European investment control regime. Instead, it aims at facilitating close and systematic cooperation among member states[39] with regard to their control mechanisms and increasing the efficiency and coherence of review procedures. Also, it shall introduce review instruments for foreign direct investments which concern specific projects or programs of Union interest.[40]

The proposed regulation provides a non-exhaustive list of factors that may be taken into account in determining whether a foreign direct investment is likely to impact public order or security.[41] In particular, the EU cautions against strategic (direct or indirect) investments by state-owned enterprises. Whether or not the investor is controlled by the government of a third country is one of the proposed screening criteria.[42] The Commission seeks to limit trade-distortive subsidization and discipline the behavior of state-owned enterprises.[43]

[39] About half of the EU member states have in place mechanisms for screening foreign direct investments, following different approaches with regard to scope and design of the screening procedures. This is the case for Austria, Denmark, Germany, Finland, France, Latvia, Lithuania, Italy, Poland, Portugal, Spain and the United Kingdom; see European Commission, *Commission Staff Working Document*, https://eur-lex.europa.eu/legal-content/EN/TXT/PDF/?uri=CELEX:52017SC0297&from=EN (accessed February 25, 2019), p. 7.

[40] European Commission, *Communication*, COM (2017) 494 final, p. 10. Assets identified as critical at the European level include Galileo, Copernicus, Eurocontrol, and the European electricity and gas transmission network. Also, EU legislation on cybersecurity lists sectors providing essential services: energy, transport, banking, financial market infrastructure, health sector, drinking water supply, and digital infrastructure and service providers; see European Commission, *Communication*, COM (2017) 494 final, p. 8.

[41] Ibid.

[42] European Commission, *Press Release, State of the Union 2017—Trade Package: Press Release, State of the Union 2017—Trade Package: European Commission proposes framework for screening of foreign direct investments*, (September 14, 2017).

[43] European Commission, *Communication*, COM (2017) 494 final, p. 6.

In June 2018, the Committee on International Trade of the European Parliament reviewed the proposal for an EU Regulation.[44] The proposal is currently being discussed in trilogues between representatives of the European Parliament, Council and Commission. The regulation is expected to come into force no earlier than 2019.

CFIUS Reform in the US

Since 1975, the Committee on Foreign Investments in the United States (CFIUS), a federal interagency committee exercising delegated presidential authority, is responsible for screening foreign investments. It is chaired by the Secretary of the Treasury and screens transactions that could result in control of a US business by a foreign person.[45] It is estimated that about 20% of CFIUS reviews over the last five or six years have involved Chinese buyers.[46]

In 2018, the US tightened its review regime by introducing "The Foreign Investment Risk Review Modernization Act of 2018" (FIRMA).[47] Among other changes, FIRMA identifies several factors that CFIUS shall take into account when considering the national security risk, extends the time limits for the review procedures, broadens the remedies at the disposal of CFIUS and—arguably the most important change—expands CFIUS' jurisdiction. While retaining the existing definition of "covered transaction" ("any merger, acquisition, or takeover that is proposed or pending [...] by or with any foreign person that could result in foreign control of any United States business"), it introduces a broad definition of "control" to include the ability to decide or direct important matters,

[44] European Parliament, *Report on the proposal for a regulation of the European Parliament and of the Council establishing a framework for screening of foreign direct investments into the European Union*, http://www.europarl.europa.eu/sides/getDoc.do?pubRef=-//EP//NONSGML+REPORT+A8-2018-0198+0+DOC+PDF+V0//EN (accessed September 21, 2018).

[45] Stephanie Zable, *The Foreign Investment Risk Review Modernization Act of 2018* (August 2, 2018), Lawfare, https://www.lawfareblog.com/foreign-investment-risk-review-modernization-act-2018 (accessed September 21, 2018).

[46] Kenneth DeWoskin, *China M&A Round-Up, Cross-border investment trends, What's the Deal? The US-China tech tug-of-war and its potential impact on M&A*, Deloitte, https://www2.deloitte.com/content/dam/Deloitte/us/Documents/mergers-acqisitions/us-ma-roundup-may-2018.pdf (accessed February 25, 2019).

[47] For the full text of the act, see https://home.treasury.gov/sites/default/files/2018-08/The-Foreign-Investment-Risk-Review-Modernization-Act-of-2018-FIRRMA_0.pdf.

whether exercised or not.[48] In addition, the bill further expands the covered transactions.[49]

Outlook

Cross-border M&A as a means for company's global growth and development, complementary to organic growth, has been discovered by Chinese companies in the recent years, though much later than the Western companies. Given the size of the Chinese economy and the globalization process Chinese companies have ahead, Chinese overseas FDI will keep growing, despite governmental restrictions both in China and in the receiving countries.

This development as an unprecedented process in world history, accompanied by the rise of China and its economy, is not a pure economic but also a political phenomenon, which is extremely exposed to domestic and global political environments, such as rising trade protectionism and in particular the tension between China and the US, and has, in return, political impact. The receiving countries will keep Chinese overseas FDI under close observation and adjust their regulation from time to time. Given the increasing significance of the economic impact of the Chinese overseas FDI, and for the interest of both sides, Chinese investors should accommodate the commercial conversions and culture of the receiving countries and make their investments more transparent regarding their motivation, strategy and financing to mitigate potential concerns in the receiving countries about their investments.

[48] Zable, *The Foreign Investment Risk Review Modernization Act of 2018*.

[49] Now included is: The purchase or lease by foreign persons of certain US real estate near a US port, military facility or other "sensitive" government property; all non-passive foreign investments in any company that deal with "critical technology", "critical infrastructure" or "sensitive personal data of United States citizens that may be exploited in a manner that threatens national security". Covered investments are those that provide corporate control, any position on the board of directors, a role in sensitive decision-making or access to "material non-public technical information", with detailed exemptions for investment funds; changes in existing ownership rights that could result in foreign ownership or control of a US business; and any other transactions structured to evade CFIUS review; see Zable, *The Foreign Investment Risk Review Modernization Act of 2018*.

CHAPTER 2

Chinese Investments in the EU

Jyrki Katainen

When we created the largest world market between 28 member states, we showed in the European Union (EU) that the free flow of ideas, goods and people can contribute decisively to achieving long-lasting peace and prosperity. Competition promotes innovation, increases the choice for consumers and reduces prices through economies of scale and specialisation. While building the EU single market, we have also paid great attention to ensuring fair competition through the adoption of strong rules against cartels, abuse of dominant positions and discipline on subsidies, and by eliminating many non-tariffs barriers between member states by adopting converging policies and standards in many fields, from agriculture to industry, services and the environment, or in basic social standards.

We believe that the same recipe that worked in the EU should work for the world. We need an open, rules-based and fair trade order. We also need global rules that promote values. Protectionism, tax evasion, dumping or low social and environmental standards are not fair or sustainable. This is why the EU supports institutions and agreements that promote this, such as the World Trade Organization (WTO), the Paris Agreement on climate change, the United Nations and the new deep and comprehensive

J. Katainen (✉)
European Commission, Brussels, Belgium
e-mail: Xavier.COGET@ec.europa.eu

T. Wenniges, W. Lohman (eds.), *Chinese FDI in the EU and the US*,
https://doi.org/10.1007/978-981-13-6071-8_2

agreements that the EU has agreed with partners such as Japan and Canada or negotiates with Mercosur.

While China initially adopted a different economic model from the 1950s to the 1970s, in the 1980s, under the influence of Deng Xiaoping, China progressively abandoned its command economy system, as it had proved unsuccessful to create durable prosperity. China leadership then accepted that a certain dose of market economy and trade openness was needed. So they changed their way of functioning, accepting private sector and entrepreneurship to a certain extent. This was a huge reform, which lasted two decades, as China was starting from very far. In the 1990s, China went one step further by acceding the WTO. They accepted lowering their custom tariffs[1] in exchange of gaining access to most of the world's markets.

The EU and other countries welcomed this change, as we want China to be prosperous economically and to join the world order that we had created. We also hoped that China would continue to open up, liberalise, move towards a full market economy and, ultimately, adopt a Western-style democratic system.

The result of Chinese economic reforms was a resounding success for China, which became the largest world exporter and the world factory. This profoundly modified the world's trade flows, and since then, the EU, the US and many other economies have experienced large and growing trade deficits with China. To a large extent, this has been because China succeeded in building a solid industrial base, had lower costs of production, cheaper labour and a virtually unlimited capacity to expand production given the size of their population and territory.

While China's economy was deeply transformed by these steps, its economic governance never fully converged towards a liberal and market economy model, as Western countries had initially hoped. In China's "*socialist market economy with Chinese characteristics*", the State actually continues to play a significant role in the economy. State-owned enterprises (SOEs) have remained strong forces in the economy, even if some consolidation and reforms have taken place to make them more efficient. Central economic planning also has continued through five-year plans, even if more flexibility has been given on how to reach objectives, and participation of the private sector along with SOEs became the norm. The

[1] China's average tariffs were of 9.9% in 2017, compared to 5.2% for the EU, 4% for Japan and 3.5% for the US in 2017 (Word Tariff Profiles 2017, WTO/ITC/UNCTAD).

Communist Party has a representative in the governance structure of private companies, and not only SOEs. And industrial policies and support schemes, including subsidies or preferential loans, continue to be rolled out to support the development of certain economic sectors.

China also has only partially opened up to foreign investment. Foreign investment is open in certain sectors, but banned in others. And for many other sectors, the situation is more blurry, with foreign investments being allowed only if done through joint ventures with a Chinese partner, within the limit of maximum equity caps, and after administrative authorisations. In many cases, this is accompanied with technology transfer requirements. This is in sheer contrasts with the situation in the EU, for instance, which is fully open to foreign investment from any source, including China, with a very few exceptions.

As time passed by, these differences in the economic systems and levels of openness between China and the West have led to the emergence of certain problems.

For instance, massive support measures and subsidies led to the accumulation of overcapacity in China in sectors such as steel and aluminium. This has generated dumping and unfair trade for EU, US and other countries' industries.

As a result, the EU, the US and many others have taken action against this in the form of anti-dumping measures on Chinese steel and aluminium imports—which are allowed by the WTO. Thanks to this, our industry has been able to survive for the time being. The problem is not over yet, though, and this is why the EU and others created a Global Forum on Steel Overcapacity in which we work together to identify and eliminate overcapacity and support measures that fuel it. Good initial results have been achieved, notably on the identification of overcapacity and how it evolves. But insufficient action has been taken to cut it. The work of the Global Forum is non-binding and its work should be expedited. It is more important than ever to do so, as overcapacity risks happening also in other sectors.

More importantly, China should actually exert more discipline and restrain on the use of subsidies and support measures when these create distortions that can harm companies abroad. First, China should abide more strictly to WTO rules on subsidies and, for example, notify fully and in detail all the subsidy schemes it has. Second, as WTO rules on subsidies are incomplete and do not cover well all situations, they should be updated. This would provide stronger discipline on massive subsidies we see in China and provide a level-playing field for all.

The EU has agreed to work with Japan and the US on this agenda. This is why we have created a trilateral cooperation on a level-playing field. We hope that China will understand the value of a strong rules-based order and join our effort, even if it means going further in the reform of their economic model.

Regarding investment flows, in spite of the restrictions on the Chinese market, EU or US businesses have massively invested in China. Some of these investments corresponded to the relocation of, for example, textile or IT production, which could be carried out more cheaply in China, and then re-exported to Western markets. In other cases, the investments were made to start production of Western products to be sold on the large Chinese markets such as cars, chemicals or pharmaceuticals. For many years, the EU has been the largest investor in China and a net capital exporter.

However, as China's economy grew, accumulated massive foreign exchange reserves, and also slowly moved up the value chain, becoming more innovative, and even more competitive than the EU in sectors such as digital and artificial intelligence, China also started exporting capital. The year 2015 was the turning point, when China became a net capital exporter, that is, invested more capital abroad than it received inland. During the first years of this new trend, China invested initially mostly in natural resources and agriculture in Asia, Africa and Latin America. However, more recently, the EU and the US became the largest destinations for Chinese foreign investments, with the acquisitions of not only infrastructure but also high-tech companies, banks and other industrial and service players.

The EU is open to foreign investment[2] because it generally creates jobs and brings technologies and know-how. However, the lack of reciprocity with China is a concern that has been raised more and more as Chinese investments continued to grow in the EU, while EU businesses continued to be subject to several limitations in China. We want to be able to invest reciprocally outside the EU as markets and value chains are global nowadays. Some have also expressed concern that certain Chinese foreign investment could be supported by subsidies, which could jeopardise the level-playing field for private investors.

[2] The EU is the world's leading source and destination of foreign direct investment (FDI), with inflows of EUR 5.7 trillion in 2015, and one of the most open economies in the world to FDI according to the OECD.

The EU has therefore first aimed at establishing a level-playing field for EU and Chinese investors by launching since 2013 negotiations of an EU-China comprehensive investment agreement that would not only protect respective investment flows but also eliminate respective barriers to investments. These negotiations, so far, however, have not yet come any close to a conclusion.

In parallel, in September 2017, the Commission proposed to create an EU foreign investment screening mechanism. There are indeed a limited number of cases where foreign direct investment (FDI) might pose a threat to security or public order. It can be the case, for example, when foreign investors seek to make investments giving them control or decisive influence on firms possessing critical technologies, critical infrastructure or sensitive information. Possible aggravating factors are situations in which the foreign investor is state owned and/or benefit from public subsidies, if this results in giving a third country influence over EU technological edge and putting EU security and public order at risk.

A theoretical possible example is the acquisition of several key energy interconnections in the EU energy network that may endanger the functioning of the Energy Union or the security of supply of certain member states. Another theoretical possible example would be the acquisition of a company possessing a key technology used for the production of sensitive military equipment.

This is why many countries have FDI screening systems in place, such as the US, China, Japan, Canada, Australia or the 12 EU member states.

The proposed Regulation for an EU FDI screening framework made in September 2017 will build on the 12 existing member states' FDI screening systems. Member states will start exchanging information on incoming FDI flows and on cases where they decide to screen specific transactions for a given reason. Member states and the European Commission will be able to comment on every screening process. But the member states in which the investment takes place will remain responsible for the final decision. No member state will be obliged to adopt an FDI screening system if it doesn't want to.

This proposal will increase the overall transparency on the issue of FDIs in the EU and on member states' FDI screening decisions, where there are some. It is important because, even though national security remains the responsibility of member states, there is also a single EU market where capital freely flows. The information sharing and cooperation system put in place will not only leave sufficient flexibility to member states to decide on their foreign investment screening policy, but also increase transparency for all and ideally promote mutual understanding and possibly convergence on foreign investment screening policy at the EU level.

The Regulation has been designed so as to avoid any negative impact on foreign investment flows to the EU, largely preserving our openness and attractiveness, and limiting administrative burden for companies.

The legislative process to adopt this proposal will last at least until mid-2019. We should ideally finalise it before the next European Parliament elections mid-2019.

To conclude, the economic rise of China is positive, as it has lifted millions of people out of poverty and allowed China to become a more prosperous country. But State influence and lack of reciprocity in market access, in particular in the field of investments, have also led to economic distortions harming EU companies and a lack of level-playing field. In order for EU-China economic relations to flourish and be mutually beneficial, it is important to address these issues. If not, contestation risks mounting. The US has notably decided to take a number of strong measures against several of the Chinese practices described above. The EU believes that there are only losers in trade wars. We therefore should work together to promote an open, rules-based and fair trade order, and upgrade it to take into account new realities, where needed. This requires commitments and actions from all, including China, which has benefited a lot from the open and rules-based multilateral system so far.

CHAPTER 3

CFIUS and a Role for American Leadership

Edwin Feulner

What is new is opposed, because most are unwilling to be taught; and what is known is rejected, because it is not sufficiently considered that men more frequently require to be reminded than informed.
—Samuel Johnson, The Rambler, *No. 2. "The Necessity and Danger of Looking into Futurity," March 1750*

Seldom before has the U.S. been so economically connected to a country it also sees as a strategic competitor. China was the U.S.'s largest trading partner in 2017, with $711 billion in cross-border trade flows. At the same time, China is highlighted in the White House's National Security Strategy document as actively challenging the U.S. in the Asia-Pacific region, globally and against Western values, and in the development of advanced technologies. The bilateral relationship is complicated to say the least. And policymakers are often unsure of how to balance economic freedom with the protection of U.S. national security from Chinese influence.

E. Feulner (✉)
The Heritage Foundation, Washington, DC, USA
e-mail: Walter.Lohman@heritage.org

T. Wenniges, W. Lohman (eds.), *Chinese FDI in the EU and the US*,
https://doi.org/10.1007/978-981-13-6071-8_3

The Committee on Foreign Investment in the U.S., or CFIUS, has been tasked for the last several decades in balancing the demand by foreign investors looking to buy American with maintaining the national security interests of the U.S. Its role is important but limited. Its greatest benefit, often going unnoticed, has been its ability to stay insulated from political influence. But its mission has become more difficult as questionable and complicated investments from countries like China have increased. Policymakers are now considering expanding the committee's authorities to counter growing competition with China. However, the difficult challenges China presents don't need difficult policies put into place. And, in fact, overburdening CFIUS could have the consequence of undermining U.S. national interests.

What the U.S. needs is a strong, flexible CFIUS that can continue to specialize in what it does best. U.S. policy should not be to unduly restrict foreign investment. For CFIUS to continue it also needs American leadership that is committed to a limited government and policymakers who have strong convictions that a free-market America is essential.

Foreign investment in the U.S. is an important feature of the global trading system. Generally speaking, other countries invest in America to access our technologies, our labor, our markets, and our "safe laws" for foreigners. What policymakers, and even investors, don't always realize is that foreign investors are actually tapping into the U.S. innovation base that has been built on the free flow of ideas and capital. And although there are still barriers to investing in the U.S., it is still the single largest destination for foreign investment in the world.

The same cannot be said for China. While foreign investment in China is growing, the seeds of foreign investment were sown in China around its entry in the World Trade Organization as American investors searched the globe for cheap manufacturing sources. China just happened to be liberalizing its economy during that time in the hopes of promoting further economic growth. To this day however, foreign investment in China has not been free. And recent debates about the trade balance between the U.S. and China has called into question the reciprocal nature of the current U.S.-China economic relationship.

The perception in Washington these days is that the U.S. government has done too little over the past two decades to manage the rise of China as a global power. It's hard to walk into an office on Capitol Hill and not, at some point, have the conversation reach a point of hyperbole and rhetoric that "the U.S. can't compete with China" and how China is "on the path to overtake America." It's fair to say less thought goes into how America has actually benefited from trading with China. What's given is that the U.S. and China are the two largest economies and trading partners in the world and, whether politicians like it or not, that's not going to change anytime soon.

Businesses and local communities, having long-wished for someone else to take action, are finding a voice in Washington. Policymakers have become so willing to take up this issue that they now risk overcompensating. What's more, some policymakers are politically incentivized to be even tougher on China than on their peers, escalating costs for those who rely so heavily on trade and international investment.

The challenges China presents are not all new. Countries under any flag are constantly competing to acquire the best resources, technology, and services for themselves. For Beijing, its investments now include moving up the value chain in manufacturing—potentially putting American jobs up against greater competition.

Many of the ongoing complaints about China aren't necessary all about China either. There is constantly a revival of debate over how technology disrupts jobs, national security, and information. These complaints are built more on the misgivings individuals have over international trade and are not China specific. Arguably, the debate over free trade has not been won—though evidence should support otherwise. Countries that have a more free economy tend to have greater prosperity. For 25 years now, the Heritage Foundation has shown how countries compare with each other in their economic freedom. But policymakers are often quick to forget the benefits of a free economy. Even policymakers from those countries that benefit the most from economic freedom decry the challenges of international competition. That being said, these days there's a growing shift in focus from national security and economic freedom to economic security.

Too often now the argument is made that economic security is national security. And that, for whatever reason, the U.S. government must strive now to protect its resources, its manufacturing base, its innovative crown jewels, its advanced services, and so on. What's taken for granted is that these innovations are not the property of the U.S. government. And U.S. national security comes from a thriving free economy, not from economic protectionism. For U.S. policymakers to pick which industries to protect is akin to the government picking from a basket the winners and losers, undermining the values meant to be protected by our national security priorities.

Policymakers generally recognize that the U.S. has some of the greatest innovators and entrepreneurs in the world. But the same policymakers sometimes lack an understanding of how the U.S. got to be so great. It's that lack of understanding American competitiveness that leads to bad policies being introduced into Congress. And much like Japanese investment was scrutinized in the 1980s by Congress, Chinese investment is similarly being scrutinized today.

U.S. policymakers are now largely concerned with the Chinese Communist Party's, "Made in China 2025" (MIC2025) industrial policy. In 2015, Beijing launched the initiative with the intention of becoming the world's leader in advanced information technology, artificial intelligence, automation, aerospace, maritime equipment, rail transport equipment, new-energy vehicles, power equipment, agricultural equipment, new materials, and advanced medical products.

U.S. policymakers tend to overestimate the abilities of foreign governments, like China's, much as they overestimate their own ability. Like most government initiatives, it is questionable how successful Beijing's MIC2025 will be. Certainly, the central and provincial governments in China will be funneling billions into these priority sectors. Many of these investments won't align with a real return on investment and therefore it will create market distortions. And for Beijing, in the long run, there will be doubts about whether the costs were worth the rewards.

Many China-watchers look at the MIC2025, and other 10- or 25-year industrial policies, with both fear and awe. The fear stems from a lack of confidence in American competitiveness. The awe comes from Beijing's ability to direct industrial policy, unlike American policymaking, which gets bogged down by politics. What policymakers don't see is that, unlike China, which is now committed to a multi-year initiative, the U.S. has flexibility in crafting new policies or abandoning ineffective ones. What's more, the U.S. innovative base doesn't have to comply with a U.S. government-mandated industrial policy. It is innovators' flexibility and ability to move about freely that's led to America's success.

But what about China? Will Beijing be able to achieve its MIC2025 goals? Rhetorically, yes. The Party will always claim a victory. But realistically, MIC2025 may help China become a competitor in a few sectors but it's unlikely to replace the U.S. and its allies as the innovative leader of the twenty-first century. Beijing's pseudo-communism, or "[s]ocialism with Chinese characteristics," still lacks what makes capitalism successful—the free flow of capital and ideas, the profit motive, and respect for the rule of law, which means insulation from corruption.

That being said, what U.S. policymakers also need to understand is that it is acceptable if the U.S. is not the leader in all economic sectors all the time. And whether China is a strategic competitor or not should not matter when it comes to making a decision of whether a specific investment in the U.S. should or should not be restricted.

Since early 2017, Congress has been looking at Chinese investment as the reason to reform CFIUS and restrict foreign investment. The complicated relationship between Washington and Beijing launched a debate on significantly broadening the committee's authority.

One argument that is made is that if China can access U.S. technology, it will recreate or copy it at home, in a cheaper, maybe better way, and in a way that undermines the products' effectiveness. And China is using any and all means available to gain U.S. technology. Strengthening of CFIUS is the leading recommendation for countering Beijing's technology acquisitions.

Currently, CFIUS reviews foreign investments and how they impact the control of a U.S. company. Control of a company, not just influence, is important because whoever is in control will determine the future of the company. If a foreign entity wants to invest in an American entity, and if that foreign investment gives the foreign entity control on the American entity, and if the American entity does business that involves U.S. national security, and if the foreign entity's investment presents a potential threat, CFIUS will consider the case. Often CFIUS gives greater scrutiny of foreign investment in technology sectors but takes a number of factors into consideration in its reviews.

When it comes to foreign investments by government-controlled entities, or state-owned enterprises (SOEs), like those controlled by the Chinese Communist Party or its People's Liberation Army, CFIUS will automatically investigate whether those investments pose a national security threat. While a Chinese company may be privately owned, there are often questions about whether financing from Chinese SOEs or Chinese policies requiring a Party member to be appointed to the company's management organization, like its board of directors, constitutes a controlling feature of the company. Thus, it can often be difficult for CFIUS to figure out who actually controls the foreign company.

Some members of Congress want to expand CFIUS's authorities in a number of ways. Some members have argued for adding food security or economic security as areas CFIUS should consider as a matter of national security. Other members want all Chinese investments to be scrutinized. Still others want CFIUS to review both how companies are controlled and how foreign investors are able to gain access to American companies, even including the American company's outbound investments.

But CFIUS, like any government bureaucracy, has limitations on what it can achieve. And CFIUS is already overwhelmed with case work. Increasing its authority to review how information is accessed is not only a logistical challenge but a diversion for the committee itself. While the committee reviews about 200 investments a year, some estimates show that proposed reforms could increase the number of reviews significantly.

Contrary to the current debate in Washington about CFIUS reform, a 2018 report by the U.S. Government Accountability Office examined CFIUS. It asked current CFIUS employees and outside experts for their thoughts on a number of CFIUS reform proposals. In general, CFIUS is managing its job well and any additional reforms are either unnecessary or risk overburdening the current committee's staff structure.

But there may be an unforeseen shift happening in CFIUS. Generally speaking, CFIUS is politically insulated, which protects the foreign investment process from transitory political pressure. It protects the free flow of investments from nebulous concepts like economic security. But CFIUS is not insulated from bureaucratic shifts in opinion as to what is considered important for U.S. national interests.

Some legitimate arguments are being made to restrict investment in technologies that have dual use between the private sector and the U.S. military. The problem here lies in determining which of those technologies are essential for the U.S. military and national security. Language in the various CFIUS reform efforts reflects a growing support for the U.S. military's third-offset strategy, which places heavy emphasis on the potential benefits of emerging technologies. The strategy places greater reliance on human-to-machine interfacing like artificial intelligence, automation, 5G telecommunications, Internet of Things, robotics, advanced manufacturing, machine learning, advanced processing, and other evolving technologies.

The changes within bureaucracy can reflect concerns over growing competition from China and its aspirations for emerging technologies. But these technologies are still developing. And according to most military experts, the U.S. has a greater problem regarding capacity, not technology.

Thus too much emphasis is being placed on emerging technologies, at a time when we don't know which emerging technologies will become essential for U.S. national interests; instead of waiting to see, policymakers could restrict who can invest in research and development. This would be akin to protecting the cart before the wheel is invented. The recent decision of CFIUS blocking a potential deal between Broadcom and Qualcomm is a good example.

So far as is publically known, China had nothing to do with the attempted acquisition of the American company Qualcomm by the Singaporean company Broadcom. We know that CFIUS decided to block this potential deal, with one of the reasons being that Qualcomm is potentially the greatest competitor with China in the development of 5G telecommunications. But this goes back to the uncertainty of emerging technology. 5G is still in development and it's questionable what the final result will look like. Hopefully, CFIUS's decision to block the deal was based on other tangible national security concerns and not an emerging U.S. industrial policy.

CFIUS review, like taxes or regulations, is a cost to investors. For some, it's a cost of uncertainty. Without CFIUS's approval, a prospective transaction could fail. More and more deals are including CFIUS provisions that require the foreign investor to reimburse the American entity if it can't clear a CFIUS review. For others, like Broadcom, it's another cost of doing business in the U.S. Like most national security efforts, the cost that CFIUS places on companies is generally accepted by the public given the potential effect some investments could have on U.S. But an overly burdensome CFIUS could potentially reduce foreign investment in the U.S., which would not be in the public's interest.

CFIUS reform should be clearly defined. It should not include intangible topics like economic security, food security, productivity, and so on. And reforms should be based on what is reasonably achievable. Having every foreign investment scrutinized over how much access is given to Chinese investors would become a bureaucratic nightmare. CFIUS could expand to consider other factors for consideration, such as how foreign investment might affect America's personal information or cybersecurity of various products and networks. And CFIUS could certainly review other types of investments such as new investments that don't require an American partner. But even these modest reforms would increase the workload of CFIUS.

It will also take strong leadership to get Congress in line with reasonable CFIUS reform. Experts should be able to identify which technologies are currently essential for U.S. national security. However, Congress continues to instruct specific federal agencies through legislation to create rules the same agencies will be enforcing. This same lack of congressional oversight goes for CFIUS reform. Congress needs to be specific in what it really wants. And what Congress should want are only those reforms that make a more effective CFIUS, not an overburdened one.

Conversations on CFIUS reform over the last several years have been a good sign that Congress can still come together for debate, even if members approach the subject from different perspectives. CFIUS reform is going to happen. The questions now are when and to what degree.

That being said, China creates challenges for American policymakers. Even so, it's questionable how effective the U.S. government can be at mitigating all of these challenges. For now, CFIUS needs to continue what it does best, just like the private sector does best without government intervention. CFIUS should continue to intervene in cases where there is a clear national security interest at stake. Otherwise, the U.S. private sector needs to be given the room to compete with foreign direct investment.

CHAPTER 4

Investment Relations with China: Never Easy but Always Worthwhile

Dieter Kempf

Foreign direct investment (FDI) is a key economic driver for both developing and advanced economies. Direct investments promote the transfer of technology and know-how, thereby increasing productivity. German industry, which is heavily export oriented and globally positioned, has always actively sought to invest in foreign markets and attract FDI. This is especially true with regard to China. For more than two decades, China has been a central destination for German FDI. Around the years 2014 and 2015, we witnessed the start of a new era of Chinese companies going global. Since then, Germany has become an important destination for Chinese FDI, mostly in the form of shareholdings or full acquisitions. But if this new era of Chinese outward FDI is to be as successful as the old one of German inward FDI, we need the right framework conditions—not least given political developments in China in recent years. The hope for an alignment of economic systems—the thesis of "change through trade"—has become a distant prospect. Indeed, we are already locked in systemic competition with China. That competition must be taken into account in the current debate on how we conduct our investment relationship with China in the future.

D. Kempf (✉)
Federation of German Industry, Berlin, Germany
e-mail: M.Schamun@bdi.eu

T. Wenniges, W. Lohman (eds.), *Chinese FDI in the EU and the US*,
https://doi.org/10.1007/978-981-13-6071-8_4

China's economic rise has been one of the most important and impressive global economic developments in the past several decades. Since its economic opening and reform process at the end of the 1970s, China has become a popular investment destination for German companies, which from 1979 onwards were able to invest in some Chinese industrial sectors by forming joint ventures with Chinese partners. In 1987 the Chinese government allowed foreign investors to establish wholly owned subsidiaries in China, albeit, once again, in a limited number of sectors. Today German direct investment is largely concentrated in the automotive sector. Other sectors with significant German investments are the chemical industry, mechanical engineering and the electrical industry.

For the Chinese government, attracting FDI has always been a means of modernising industrial sectors through foreign technology, capital, management skills and expertise. From the outset, its policies towards FDI have been intended to guide investment into targeted industries while protecting strategic interests. Following China's accession to the World Trade Organization (WTO) in 2001, other industries were opened up to foreign investment. It is indisputable that foreign investors have made a huge contribution to China's economic development, especially since most FDI into China is greenfield and therefore has a much larger positive impact on job creation compared to mergers and acquisitions. These investments allowed for a massive transfer of technology and best practices, but also had spillover effects into the service sector and other industries. In exchange, China offered favourable production conditions, low labour costs and enormous domestic market prospects.

However, while the total stock of European FDI in China further increased, annual investment inflows from Europe to China have declined somewhat in recent years. During the period 2010–2015, annual European FDI in China was around €10 billion, but in 2016–2018 it fell to €8 billion. One of the reasons for that decline has been the more difficult economic environment: growth is still on a high level, but slowing, and wages are rising. Competition from Chinese companies is getting fiercer but business barriers for foreign companies still remain high. The sluggish progress of market reforms acts as another brake on investment growth. And China is still imposing significant market access restrictions on foreign companies.

Despite these challenges, China's domestic market and its economic development continue to offer great potential for European investors.

Among the reasons for us to remain optimistic are the high Chinese gross domestic product (GDP) growth rates (which remain far above those of most industrialised countries), China's population of 1.4 billion and its growing middle class. Moreover, there are reasons to hope that China will further open its markets to foreign investors.

China Goes Global

For a long time, investment flows between the European Union (EU)/ Germany and China were largely a one-way street. Not much changed after the Chinese government unveiled its "going out" strategy in 2000. But meanwhile, after three decades of being primarily a recipient of FDI, China has emerged as a major FDI-originating country. It is no longer the case that Chinese investment in the EU is virtually non-existent, as was the situation until recently.

The last ten years especially have seen China's financial reach rapidly extend beyond its borders. Today, many Chinese companies are investing and operating abroad. Beijing encourages Chinese enterprises, backed by China's huge foreign exchange reserves, to acquire assets and expand business overseas. While Chinese outbound FDI was initially focused on natural resource extraction in developing economies, that focus has shifted in recent years to advanced economies, including the countries of the EU. The 2007–2011 financial and economic crisis yielded opportunities to acquire European companies at relatively low prices, and Chinese entrepreneurs were spurred to invest in the European market by the desire to secure a stronger foothold in the world's second-largest consumer market, the strength of the European R&D landscape and the availability of highly skilled workers.

In the case of Germany, the quality guarantee "Made in Germany" and the country's central geographical location in Europe certainly add to its attractiveness as an investment destination. When Chinese companies started to invest in Europe on a larger scale, investments from China were seen by most Germans as providing new impetus for development and promoting the opening of the Chinese market to German companies, some of which were struggling owing to structural problems and insufficient capital. That impression derived not least from German companies that had switched to Chinese ownership in the past, enjoying various advantages under their new owners, including employment guarantees, a long-term commitment to the location and improved access to the Chinese market. And besides the economic advantages, many in Germany had hoped at the time that increasing interconnectedness would lead to the convergence of economic systems.

Since the Chinese leadership transition in 2012, we have seen a change in the investment behaviour of Chinese investors. China's "going out" strategy is itself undergoing major change: since industrial upgrade is one of President Xi Jinping's top priorities, the focus of the "going out" strategy has shifted to the acquisition of foreign technology so that China can move up the industrial value chain. This national target is prominently laid out in the "Made in China 2025" strategy, which focuses on key industries Chinas planners believe will dominate the economic landscape of the future. In this context, Germany is a particularly popular investment destination, as it has many privately owned small- and medium-sized enterprises—"hidden champions"—which are attractive targets for Chinese companies seeking technology leadership. In recent years, there have been share purchases in companies such as EEW Energy from Waste (Beijing Enterprises), KrausMaffei (ChemChina) and Bilfinger SE Wassertechnik (Chengdu Techcent Environment Group), as well as the takeover of the banking house Hauck & Aufhäuser by the conglomerate Fosun. Acquisitions or purchases of further shares in recent years include industry leaders Putzmeister by Sany and KION (45 per cent share) by Weichai Power.

Still a Win-Win Situation?

While initially most Germans were well inclined towards Chinese direct investments, a debate has since emerged over whether the impact of Chinese investments in Germany is mainly positive or negative. That debate was fueled in 2016 by the announced plans of the Chinese company Midea to take over the German robot manufacturer KUKA. Since then, concerns have grown that Germany could lose competitiveness in key industries by selling enterprises to China. At the same time, warnings have been sounded that the functioning of market mechanisms could be weakened—since Chinese investors are both willing and able to pay prices that do not reflect market prices as they are estimated by Western companies. This fact also raises questions about "unfair doping" in the form of state help.

Moreover, fears were expressed at the time of the planned KUKA takeover that the German government did not have sufficient administrative instruments to control risks arising from acquisitions by Chinese companies. In mid-July 2017 the German government amended the

Foreign Trade and Payment Ordinance (AWV) to expand the list of economic sectors in which takeovers are subject to approval and to extend the review period. This was followed by another amendment in December 2018 lowering the bar for a screening in some instances to a share of 10 per cent. Thus, for reasons of national security, it can now block FDI not only in the German defence industry but also in "critical infrastructure". On the EU level a joint action by three countries pushed forward the issue. In February 2017 Germany, France and Italy sent a letter to the EU Trade Commissioner Cecilia Malmström requesting for the adoption of political measures aimed at greater reciprocity between EU member and non-member countries in market access for FDI and access to procurement markets. This initiative set in motion a process that was finalised two years later, in Spring 2019, with the adoption of a new regulation on state control of foreign investment by the European Parliament. In essence this new regulation is a step in the right direction. It meets two central requirements of the German industry. Firstly, interventions may only be made to protect national security and secondly, the decision on investment bans remains in the power of the member states. This will help curb the politicisation of investment controls.

The Federation of German Industries' (BDI, Bundesverband der Deutschen Industrie) position on foreign investment is clear: Foreign investors—including those from China—are welcome in Germany and the EU. Their investments create wealth and jobs. The fundamental freedom of investment must be maintained in the EU. Property rights and freedom of contract must also be guaranteed and strengthened as fundamental pillars of the liberal and social market economy in Germany. Deviations from these principles may only occur in a few clearly defined areas. The "protection of public order and security", as regulated in the Foreign Trade and Payments Law (AWG) and the Foreign Trade and Payments Ordinance, is a generally accepted criterion for state intervention in investment decisions. A problem, however, is the worldwide trend that governments are increasingly expanding the concept of national security in order to limit "access" of foreign investors to technologies deemed worthy of protection. Therefore, the investment audit mechanism anchored in German foreign trade law should continue to be strictly limited and exclude any economic factors. Apart from issues of national security, the BDI and its members share concerns which include possible distortions of competition through state-subsidised takeovers. In order to prevent distortions of competition on the takeover market, adjustments should instead be made to competition law, not foreign trade law. EU competition instruments do not, or only to a very limited extent, address market-distorting practices or target state support brought into the EU internal market from outside. This is currently putting our businesses at a competitive disadvantage. The BDI therefore calls for a stronger use of competition policy in order to ensure a level-playing field in investment.

On the other hand, China could do its part by ensuring more transparency with regard to financing conditions, corporate accounting standards and ownership structures. That would narrow the gap and go a long way towards restoring acceptance of Chinese investments in Europe.

Chinese Investors: Different from Most Others

That said, China is making it difficult for us to apply a light-touch regulatory approach towards Chinese investments. While governments should intervene in private investment decisions on economic grounds only when markets are distorted—even some proponents of openness and minimal state intervention admit that market distortion is intolerable—we cannot but acknowledge that it is not always easy to determine whether an investor is playing by the rules. And this is particularly true for China, where ownership structures and funding sources are often non-transparent and the dividing line between the state and business is blurred. Moreover, the argument that "[w]e don't want to become 'Chinese' by closing our own market to foreign investors" weighs heavily in the current debate.

Various aspects of both the Chinese economy and Chinese politics underscore that China is an investor unlike any other. This does not mean that we do not want investments from China in Europe. Nevertheless, we must be aware of those features that are peculiar to China and take them into account in the current discussion:

- *Asymmetries in market access*: A huge challenge related to Chinese FDI is the lack of reciprocity. The European Union Chamber of Commerce in China had good reason to ask the following question in its 2017/2018 position paper on European business in China: "Does [China] support only one-way investment openness that allows its enterprises to go global while foreign business, sitting on China's doorstep, is again told to be patient?" EU countries have largely open investment regimes, with few explicit restrictions on investment. Chinese companies face few, if any, limitations in investing in European industries such as automotive, construction, financial services, healthcare, insurance, logistics, media and telecommunications. By contrast, European companies in China continue to be either barred from participating in those industries or limited to holding a minority position. Free movement of capital is one of the "four freedoms" of the EU single market: it requires all EU member states to allow unhindered capital flows not only between member states but also from third countries into the EU market. For its part, Germany has traditionally adopted an open investment stance by offering foreign investors free market access and refraining from use of a general protection mechanism for key technologies. It offers complete freedom in terms of greenfield investments and has only a small number of restrictions on national security grounds with regard to mergers and acquisitions.

This is not the case in China. An index of market access restrictiveness compiled by the Organisation for Economic Co-operation and Development (OECD) suggests that China remains among those countries with the most restricted access for foreign investors. The Chinese government protects strategic industries from foreign access, which means that European businesses in China encounter numerous barriers—both formal and informal—of a political and legal nature. Entire Chinese sectors are closed to foreign investment and a number of industries are subject to joint venture coercion. China prohibits foreign investment in a number of sectors and severely restricts it in other areas. And it continues to do so despite having become a major advocate of globalisation and free trade in its rhetoric and repeatedly asserting that it wants to open up to foreign investors and will make the necessary changes.

In early 2017 China amended its "Catalogue for the Guidance of Foreign Investment Industries", which was launched in 1995 in order to "guide" FDI into Chinese industry. As a result of those amendments, the number of sectors restricted to foreign investment has been reduced from 93 to 63. However, that reduction was partially on paper only: in reality, just 18 sectors can be considered to have been removed from the catalogue's "negative list" and opened up to some extent. The hopes of foreign companies were further fueled by the so-called State Council Document No. 5 or Circular No. 5 (Notice on Several Measures on Promoting Further Openness and Active Utilisation of Foreign Investment), which was released at the beginning of 2017. That document outlines three policy goals: (1) take further steps to open up to the outside world, (2) further create an environment of fair competition, and (3) further strengthen efforts to attract foreign investment. In 2018, China announced several rounds of tariff cuts. Most prominently, it lowered import tariffs to 15 per cent on autos and components, from 25 per cent for passenger cars and 20 per cent on trucks, followed by further cuts on import taxes covering more than 700 goods. The cuts mainly targeted products which China regarded as benefiting the own economy or lowering costs for domestic consumers. Beyond that, China presented its long announced "negative list" for foreign investment, eventually replacing the former "Catalogue for the Guidance of Foreign Investment Industries" and reducing the number of restricted or forbidden sectors by 15 to 48. In another step, the National Development and Reform Commission published its first national negative list for investment, specifying 151 areas that are either banned to non-state businesses or require government approval for entry. Some of the mentioned steps were regarded as "window-dressing" or long overdue, but it also must be acknowledged, that they are a move in the right direction. The announcement of ending the joint venture constraint in the coming years for the production of cars, aircrafts and ships is one such positive example. Some German car makers have already taken the opportunity to extend their share with their Chinese Joint Venture Partners of up to 75 per cent. Nonetheless, there are still too many restrictions on investment as well as high tariffs and non-tariff barriers in place. Some argue, that without the pressure of a looming trade war with the United States, China wouldn't have been so quick in implementing these measures, and in China voices were heard that outside pressure on reforms would strengthen the position of the liberal and market-oriented groups within the Chinese authorities. In 2019, the new Foreign Direct Investment Law could be the next big step in favor of foreign companies, depending on how it will be enforced in practice. According to the draft, government officials will be prohibited from using administrative means to force foreign businesses to transfer their technology and foreign investors could enjoy equal treatment with domestic counterparts, with the exception of sectors specified in the government's negative list. As promising as those policy goals sound, German industry would welcome faster and more decisive implementation. The asymmetry in openness was tolerable as long as investments flowed mainly in one direction, but since China has become the second-largest global investor after the United States and a technological powerhouse, it is no longer sustainable—neither politically nor economically.

- *Systemic competition and market distortion*: The EU provides conditions for open, market-based international competition. China, on the other hand, is a "socialist market economy" in which the state enjoys extensive rights to intervene in the market. Informal interrelationships exist between the state and the economy in China and market distortions result from state ownership, state subsidies and other non-market economic features. State-owned enterprises have traditionally played a major role in the Chinese economy—a role that has grown not weaker but stronger in recent years—and today they are important investors abroad. It is true that, in general, it is very difficult to differentiate between state and private players in FDI; but this is especially the case in China, where even formal ownership structures often lack transparency. Chinese FDI continues to grow without any clear separation between the authorities and domestic commercial entities. That party cells are being established or revived in companies and joint ventures suggests that the Chinese state has no intention whatsoever of withdrawing from the economy. However, in the current debate about investment screening, China has spoken out strongly against any more state intervention in Europe.
- *Strategy for innovation*: Investment is always closely linked to innovation. Ideally, investment encourages innovation. In Germany, the state promotes and supports applied research in industry based on the common belief that new technologies and new products are most efficiently developed and marketed by industry. All market participants are treated equally—regardless of whether they are German, European or non-European. Meanwhile, China, on the other hand, has drawn up a state innovation plan with clear targets aimed at promoting its high-tech sectors. In practice, substantial government research funds are available mainly to Chinese companies. Under its "Made in China 2025" strategy, which was introduced in 2015, China has developed a new long-term industrial strategy. The strategy identifies the high-tech industries in which it wants to compete internationally through its own companies. The aim is to achieve

global leadership in various key technologies (including information technology, computer-controlled machines, industrial robots, energy-saving vehicles and medical devices) by 2049. China is moving up the global value chain and ridding itself of the image of the "cheap workbench of the world"; indeed, it is fast becoming a high-tech superpower and clearly sees technology acquisition through outward FDI as an important tool to expedite this process. This strategy is problematic—for two reasons. First, it is neither an effective nor a sustainable way to improve competitiveness and boost the innovative capacity of Chinese industry as a whole. A much more effective approach would be to create the right framework conditions for China's domestic market. Second, it causes friction with China's trading partners and hinders fair global competition, and may in the end lead to more state intervention on all sides—not least owing to the above-mentioned asymmetries in market access.

For decades, another integral part of China's innovation strategy has been forced technology transfer—that is, granting market access in exchange for technology. This practice takes place via joint ventures, public tendering, certification practices and investment permits. German industry is very interested in an innovative and strong China, as our closest trade links are with other high-tech countries; accordingly, China's development as a high-tech location promises to offer many opportunities. However, those opportunities will materialise only if foreign companies are given the same opportunities to participate as local companies. We need a level-playing field, a predictable regulatory framework and a free exchange of ideas and data. This last factor is particularly important, as digitisation will play an increasing role for our economies.

Minimise Risks, Maximise Opportunities

Given the enduring systemic differences between the EU's open market economy and China's "socialist market economy", it is clear that the regulatory framework for our investment relations has to adequately address those differences in order to minimise the risks and maximise the opportunities. Systemic competition persists between the Chinese economy with its central planning and the Western market economy, in which economic planning is largely the responsibility of private enterprises. This competition can be won only with the help of the principles of our open market system. We cannot respond to Chinese central planning by dismantling the open market economy, which, based on the principles of private property and freedom of contract, is a much stronger mechanism for promoting innovation and discovering new knowledge than is central planning. Therefore, the protection of the open market system, rather than the protection of technologies, is key for Europe to remain competitive in the next decades. We must strengthen the basic market economic principles rather than weaken them. And for that reason, we must proceed carefully with expanding the scope of foreign investment screening.

We believe that the best way forward would be a comprehensive bilateral investment treaty between the EU and China that gives investors predictable, long-term access to the respective markets and protects both investors and their investments in those markets. Especially important, the treaty should ensure equal market access for German companies in China and for Chinese companies in the EU. German subsidiaries in China should enjoy the same entrepreneurial freedom of action as do Chinese domestic companies. Unfortunately, since their beginning in 2013, the treaty negotiations have yet to show fundamental progress. As the asymmetries in market access are a big disadvantage for European companies on the global competition landscape, our strong hope is that the negotiations will progress and come to a completion in the foreseeable future A clear concession from China towards opening its markets would send a powerful signal. Moreover, it would keep the new global wave of protectionism at bay and make it easier for those committed to an open investment regime in Europe.

References

Bundesverband der Deutschen Industrie (BDI) (2017a), Requirements of a Bilateral Investment Treaty Between the EU and China; Berlin, August.

Bundesverband der Deutschen Industrie (BDI) (2017b), Expanding the Scope of Foreign Investment Screenings of non-EU investors; Berlin, July.

Bundesverband der Deutschen Industrie (BDI) (2019), China–Partner and Systemic Competitor. How Do We Deal With China's State-Controlled Economy? Berlin.

European Union Chamber of Commerce in China (EUCCC) (2017), European Business in China, Position Paper 2017/2018, Beijing.

Hanemann, Thilo; Huotari, Mikko (2018), EU-China FDI: Working towards reciprocity in investment relations, MERICS Papers on China, Berlin.

Jungbluth, Cora (2016), Chance und Herausforderung. Chinesische Direktinvestitionen in Deutschland; Global Economic Dynamics Studie, Gütersloh, Bertelsmann Stiftung.

Strack, Friedolin (2017), Die Sicht der deutschen Industrie auf chinesische Hochtechnologie-Investitionen in Deutschland, Policy Brief, Bonn, Deutsches Zentrum für Luft- und Raumfahrt.

CHAPTER 5

Averting Conflict by Promoting Commerce: The Case for a U.S.-China Investment Treaty

Peter Goettler and Daniel Ikenson

Introduction

The problems besetting the U.S.-China economic relationship today predate Donald Trump. They originate as the frictions one should expect when an incumbent economic power is compelled to accommodate the emergence of a rising challenger. Of course, Trump's caustic approach to commercial and diplomatic relations threatens to worsen bilateral ties, but it also could shake things up enough to yield solutions to some of the most pressing problems.

During China's dramatic rise from a near-subsistence economy in 1978 to the world's manufacturing powerhouse by 2008, frictions were aplenty. But they were managed reasonably well. Over the past ten years, as the United States struggled to shake off the economic and psychological effects of the Great Recession and China refocused its priorities on closing the technological gap, U.S. policymakers grew increasingly wary of Beijing's aims and tactics. With occasional frictions becoming persistent sources of tension, many in Washington no longer consider China an economic rival, but an adversary.

P. Goettler • D. Ikenson (✉)
CATO Institute, Washington, DC, USA
e-mail: DIkenson@cato.org

T. Wenniges, W. Lohman (eds.), *Chinese FDI in the EU and the US*,
https://doi.org/10.1007/978-981-13-6071-8_5

It is against this backdrop that Donald Trump arrived in Washington in 2017 with his unorthodox economic views and his penchant for incendiary rhetoric. President Trump's confrontational approach to problems both real and imagined has heightened tensions with China, pushing the world's two largest economies into a trade war. In 2018, Trump imposed tariffs on $250 billion of imports from China, and Beijing responded with tariffs on $130 billion of U.S. imports. As of this writing, U.S. and Chinese negotiators are reportedly close to reaching a deal that will lift at least some of the tariffs. Presumably, the terms of any deal will include commitments from China to change certain objectionable practices and purchase more U.S. products. But whether the tariffs will be lifted on all products immediate or some products gradually or something in between remains unclear.

The motivation for Trump's tariffs—though not a legitimate justification for acting unilaterally and subverting the international trade rules—is China's industrial policies in the technology space, which presumably hurt U.S. companies and threaten U.S. security. Moreover, accumulating frictions over trade imbalances, trade rule violations, market-distorting industrial policies, discriminatory treatment of foreign companies, and other forms of emerging trade and investment protectionism are weighing on the relationship. But rather than the United States imposing self-destructive tariffs as a "remedy" and China responding with self-destructive tariffs as retaliation, Washington and Beijing should consider more constructive alternatives, since a stable and growing commercial relationship is important to the well-being of the U.S., Chinese, and global economies.

Both governments have gripes—some of which are valid concerns about the policies of the other. And, presumably, both governments would prefer to resolve these problems through negotiations instead of a deleterious trade war. Accordingly, the U.S. and Chinese governments—recognizing that tariff put us on a ruinous path that may be difficult to unwind—should catalogue all of their concerns, put them on the table, and see whether and to what extent they can be resolved or mitigated in a bilateral trade or investment agreement.

An Investment Treaty?

Valued at more than $700 billion, the U.S.-China trade relationship gets a lot of attention in the media and among policymakers.[1] Often the attention is focused on the fact that the trade account (or the slightly broader

[1] Bureau of the Census, Import and Export Statistics.

"current account") is "out of balance." With U.S. entities importing over $520 billion of goods and services in 2017, while exporting only $180 billion, President Trump and others view the resulting $340 billion deficit as an indication that the United States is on the losing end of this relationship and believe this is because the Chinese are cheating.[2]

But that conclusion betrays a lack of understanding of the dynamics of global trade and investment flows. When the current account is in deficit, the capital account is in surplus by a perfectly offsetting amount. The sum of the United States' current account deficit and its capital account surplus is zero, which means that the value of U.S. purchases of goods, services, and assets *from* foreigners equals the value of U.S. sales of goods, services, and assets *to* foreigners. Put another way, when Americans buy more goods and services from foreigners than they sell to them (a current account deficit), then the value of U.S. assets purchased by foreigners exceeds the value of foreign assets purchased by Americans (a capital account surplus) by an equally offsetting amount.

Of course, this balance is the result of an accounting identity that always holds at the global level, but not necessarily at the bilateral level. But America's large trade deficit with China (as meaningless as bilateral trade accounting is in a globalized economy) is attended by a large capital account surplus with China. That inward investment helps fuel U.S. economic growth.

At $1.63 trillion in 2017, Chinese holdings of U.S. assets are heavily weighted toward public and private securities, especially U.S. government debt.[3] With a portfolio valued at $1.19 trillion, China is the largest foreign holder of U.S. treasury securities.[4] And while relatively small at present, Chinese investors in recent years have begun to diversify their U.S. asset portfolios by purchasing U.S. companies and establishing commercial entities in the United States. At the end of 2017, the stock of Chinese foreign direct investment (FDI) in the United States was valued at $58 billion.[5]

The matter of Chinese acquisitions of U.S. companies has become a more volatile component of the bilateral relationship in recent years, however. Growing concerns among U.S. policymakers about the national

[2] Ibid.

[3] Wayne M. Morrison, "China-U.S. Trade Issues," Congressional Research Service Report, July 30, 2018.

[4] Ibid.

[5] Ibid.

security implications of Chinese purchases—especially of U.S. technology companies—has led to calls for more rigorous U.S. government controls over the process, as well as a broadening of the types of transactions that should be subject to government review and approval.

Last month, committees in both chambers of Congress unanimously approved bills that would greatly expand the authority of the U.S. Committee on Foreign Investment in the United States (CFIUS), which is a multiagency review board that considers prospective foreign acquisitions of U.S. companies and advises the president—who can block the deal—of any national security risks presented by the transaction. The intention of both bills is to expand the definition of "covered transactions" so that certain kinds of investments that have eluded scrutiny in the past will fall under the purview of CFIUS, which will be empowered to apply more rigorous standards of review to prospective acquisitions from certain countries, including China.[6]

A constant refrain from President Trump is that the United States is on the losing end of economic relationships because previous U.S. presidents and their negotiators never insisted on "reciprocity" with respect to reducing tariffs or barriers to investment, and demands for reciprocity with respect to market access for goods, services, and investment have grown louder in Washington. While we certainly support the concept and goal of reciprocity, proper analysis of trade policy requires a recognition that the U.S. economy and aggregate U.S. wealth benefits from imports and investment from China *regardless* of whether U.S. exports and investment to China are permitted reciprocally. So imposing tariffs, import restrictions, or other protectionist measures in pursuit of reciprocity is self-defeating. And because inbound investment is essential to domestic economic activity, the threat of cutting off imports and inbound investment unless and until exports and outbound investment are permitted on reciprocal terms lacks credibility. Nevertheless, outbound investment is essential to the competitiveness of domestic businesses operating in foreign markets.

While overall Chinese investment in the United States vastly exceeds overall U.S. investment in China, the stock of U.S. direct investment in China amounted to $92 billion at the end of 2017 (exceeding China's $58 billion of FDI in the United States). That fact notwithstanding, U.S.

[6] See the Foreign Investment Risk Review Modernization Act (S. 2098/H.R. 4311, FIRRMA for short).

businesses report facing a variety of barriers to investment in China. Sectors comprising large portions of the Chinese economy remain off limits to foreign investment, and those that are nominally opened can be accessed only upon the foreign entity meeting a variety of often-onerous performance requirements. In China, U.S. businesses seek broader investment access to the market on more transparent, predictable, nondiscriminatory terms.

China cordons off many domestic sectors from foreign direct investment, including banking, life insurance services, securities and asset management services, agriculture, mining, and certain parts of manufacturing. According to the U.S.-China Business Council, China imposes ownership barriers on nearly 100 industries.[7]

China maintains onerous rules, including caps on foreign equity, joint venture requirements, forced technology transfers, local research and development mandates, content requirements, minimum export requirements, opaque national security and cybersecurity compliance procedures, a case-by-case administrative approval system for certain investments, and a maze of licensing requirements. U.S. entities have raised concerns over the years about China's restrictive investment environment, but that has produced only limited relaxation of the many restrictions.[8]

The Organisation for Economic Co-operation and Development (OECD) maintains and publishes a FDI restrictiveness database which gauges "the restrictiveness of a country's foreign direct investment (FDI) rules by looking at four main types of restrictions: foreign equity restrictions; discriminatory screening or approval mechanisms; restrictions on key foreign personnel; and operational restrictions." Restrictiveness indices are produced for all 34 OECD countries and 33 non-OECD countries. The index is a composite of measurements of nine component sectors of each country's economy and provides a general overview of the investment environment (although effective implementation, enforcement, exercise of discretion, and degree of transparency also matter, but are not reflected in the scores).

Of the 67 countries assessed, China has the fourth most restrictive investment regime, with a score of 0.316 in 2017—on a scale of 0 (open) to 1 (closed). The United States, while scoring a much more open 0.089,

[7] U.S.-China Business Council, China's WTO Compliance, September 20, 2013.

[8] https://ustr.gov/sites/default/files/files/Press/Reports/China%202017%20WTO%20Report.pdf.

still comes in below the OECD average of 0.066.[9] Ownership restrictions in U.S. fisheries, utilities, maritime and air transportation, and radio and television industries help explain why the United States isn't closer to 0.0.[10]

Establishing a presence in the world's most populous country—soon to be the largest economy—is essential to commercial success there, and an important component of many businesses' global strategy. In 2015 (the most recent year for which data are available), Chinese affiliates of U.S.-headquartered companies accounted for $481 billion of sales in China—quadruple the value of U.S. exports to China that year.[11] Succeeding in the Chinese market is about much more than simply exporting goods to China. Having a domestic presence to provide services, oversee distribution, provide after-market support, conduct market research, and cultivate brand identity is essential to success. And if U.S. companies are able to compete and succeed in China, they are more likely to succeed at home and around the world.

By the same token, the Chinese government should be welcoming U.S. direct investment with open arms. In 2015, U.S. affiliates in China employed 2.1 million workers, paid $35 billion in employment compensation, and spent $3.4 billion on research and development.[12] Not only do these investment inflows create value-added and employment opportunities, but they bring best business practices that can be adopted, modified, and adapted to Chinese business customs.

But recent surveys by U.S. (and European) business groups reflect growing concern among multinational companies about an unpredictable and "increasingly hostile" investment and business climate in China, which is perpetually tilted in favor of domestic enterprises.

U.S. trade officials have urged China to liberalize its FDI regime in order to boost U.S. business opportunities in, and expand U.S. exports to, China. To that end, the United States and China began contemplating a bilateral investment treaty in 2008, but it wasn't until 2013 that a framework for a modern agreement was established. After a few years of modest progress, it became apparent by the end of the Obama administration that Washington and Beijing were too far apart for a deal to come to fruition

[9] https://data.oecd.org/fdi/fdi-restrictiveness.htm.

[10] https://www.cato.org/publications/policy-analysis/reversing-worrisome-trends-how-attract-retain-investment-competitive.

[11] Congressional Research Service.

[12] Bureau of Economic Analysis, Activities of U.S. Affiliates of Foreign Multinational Enterprises, 2016, www.bea.gov.

in the near term. According to U.S. officials, the Chinese were unwilling to reduce the number of industries it was insisting would be off limits to foreign investment. While threatening or starting a trade war is a dangerous—and potentially costly—tactic to stimulate desired changes in trade relationships, the looming specter of escalating trade disruptions may have changed China's calculus on this issue: there may be greater receptivity to ideas that can help both sides avert such outcomes.

Simple Investment Rules for a Complex Investment Relationship

A proper bilateral investment treaty should employ a "negative list" approach to open all sectors (or nearly all—with limited exceptions for those that are most sensitive) of both economies to investment from businesses and nationals of the other country. That means that commitments made by the parties apply to all sectors and activities that are not explicitly identified as exemptions ("on the negative list"). This approach is more liberalizing because any new industries that emerge will be already excluded from the list and are automatically open to foreign investment. Moreover, the existence of a list of sectors that remain protected readily identifies industries that might be targeted for future reforms.

The treaty should prohibit the use of "performance requirements," including local content requirements, minimum export requirements, technology transfer, joint venture, localization, and any similar performance-restraining requirements as conditions of investment. It should obligate parties not to impede the flow of capital related to investments, including transfers of profits, dividends, interest payments, and royalties. The treaty should guarantee the rights of investors to appoint senior managers without regard to nationality and require that any restrictions on the appointment of board members based on nationality do not adversely affect an investor's control of their investment.

By contributing to an environment that ensures greater transparency and predictability based on the rule of law, these provisions make investment treaties worthwhile. Juxtaposed against the specter of metastasizing trade and investment restrictions, an investment treaty could restore faith in the relationship and improve prospects for realizing previously untapped benefits.

Non-discrimination requirements, under which parties agree to treat foreign investors and investments as they would domestic investors and investments, are also an important component of investment treaties. Accordingly, the treaty should include basic guarantees and protections for investors and investments, including the right to "national treatment," a "minimum standard of treatment," and rights to compensation for government expropriation of an investment.

Investment treaties often include provisions entitling the parties to pursue neutral arbitration of disputes in international tribunals under the terms of provisions known as investor-state dispute settlement (ISDS). The ostensible purpose of ISDS is to ensure that foreign investors are protected against host government actions or policies that fail to meet certain standards of treatment and that cause the investor economic harm. Examples would be changes in laws, regulations, or procedures that have a discriminatory effect on foreign investors and which cause financial harm—these are the kinds of claims brought to ISDS arbitration.

While a mechanism to provide such protections may seem reasonable, ISDS provisions are market distorting and, potentially, sovereignty usurping. Because of these and a variety of other downsides—which could be plumbed here only at the expense of taking this analysis off course—ISDS provisions should not be included in a U.S.-China investment treaty. With reference to a previous Cato Institute paper for the details, suffice it to say that the absence of ISDS provisions hasn't dissuaded U.S. companies from investing in China.[13]

Conclusion

As perverse as it may seem, the specter of escalating tariffs, investment restrictions, and a destructive trade war may be creating an opportunity for the United States and China to return to their suspended bilateral investment treaty negotiations and execute an agreement. The negotiations that began under President Obama in 2013 produced a framework for an agreement that could conceivably resolve some persistent issues.

[13] Daniel Ikenson, "A Compromise to Advance the Trade Agenda," Cato Free Trade Bulletin No. 57, March 4, 2014.

To address and possibly resolve some old and emerging problems that threaten to inflict lasting damage on the bilateral relationship, Washington and Beijing have much to gain from an agreement that offers new business opportunities and supports the rule of law and enhanced transparency.

CHAPTER 6

The Significance of Chinese Financial Market Liberalisation

Joachim Wuermeling

Introduction

The expression "new era" carries particular magnitude. Whenever a development comes along which promises to permanently alter the lives of many people, we speak of a new era. This is why there was good reason to prick our ears when the president of China, Xi Jinping, spoke of a new era recently. According to President Xi, one major element of this new era is that China is opening up—and he expressly included the financial markets. So it's no surprise, then, that China's central bank and finance ministry have been emitting clear signals in favour of more bidirectional financial flows. As a case in point, the foreign ownership limits in Chinese financial institutions have recently been relaxed, and the schemes to liberalise the cross-border capital flows have received further push by raised quotas.

From a European vantage point, one might initially wonder what is so pioneering about the opening-up of financial markets. After all, as some will note, open financial markets are one of the salient features of the EU single market, and have been so for a quarter of a century. But open

J. Wuermeling (✉)
German Central Bank, Frankfurt, Germany
e-mail: oliver.loch@bundesbank.de

T. Wenniges, W. Lohman (eds.), *Chinese FDI in the EU and the US*,
https://doi.org/10.1007/978-981-13-6071-8_6

financial markets in Europe have not always been a cut-and-dried affair. We conveniently overlook the fact that only since 1993, with the Treaty of Maastricht, all restrictions on the movement of capital between Member States and between Member states and third countries were prohibited. But a quarter of a century after this, the European financial markets are still fragmented in some segments. That is why a capital markets union [—a project dating back to 2015—], which the Bundesbank also supports, is intended to realign these markets more closely by 2019.

So it's worth taking a fresh, unprejudiced look at the following questions: What are the pros and cons for China of opening up its financial markets? Why is this country seeking to open up further? To answer these questions, we will shed light on some findings from the literature first and then contrast them with experience from the Asian crisis, which left its mark on China, amongst other countries. We will continue by discussing how the potential future role of China's currency, the renminbi, could be an engine of further financial market liberalisation.

Main Part

Advantages of Open Financial Markets in the Literature

The advantages of open financial markets in the traditional textbook literature appear intuitive. Let us list three of these theoretical foundations. First: economies are rewarded for opening themselves up to cross-border capital flows with better growth opportunities. Open financial markets, in principle, support economic growth by enabling resources to be directed to their most productive uses. In saving rich countries—like China—they create broader investment opportunities for savers, thereby increasing aggregate yields (and possibly allowing to save less and free some resources for consumption). Capital inflows can reduce firms' funding costs and thus spur investment. The result is higher, and more productive, investment, and more dynamic growth, than absent the free movement of capital.

Second: open financial markets encourage greater market discipline. At the microeconomic level, increased competition with non-residents forces domestic financial institutions to be more efficient, more transparent, and better governed. In macroeconomic terms, open financial markets and the attendant competition for global funding provide incentives for institutional reforms, such as to legal systems and legal certainty, accounting and disclosure standards. Domestic financial supervisors can benefit from knowledge transfer by obtaining a deeper insight into foreign institutions' risk management practices. Anyone who takes a little time to read up on the Chinese financial system will soon realise that this is another angle from which China stands to benefit both microeconomically and macroeconomically from a further opening-up of financial markets.

Third: open financial markets open the door to stability gains through cross-border risk-sharing. Investors have more options for diversifying their portfolios across multiple countries, giving them an insurance of sorts against a shock striking their own country. This is because, if their home country falls into recession, the lower income from domestic assets can be compensated for by returns on foreign investments not affected by the recession. Consumption fluctuations can thus be dampened to a certain degree. China's avowed goal of "rebalancing" its economy from one that tends to be investment- and export-driven to one that is more strongly consumption- and services-oriented represents an additional incentive to take larger, more dynamic steps towards financial market liberalisation.

Practical Experience of Open Financial Markets During the Asian Crisis

In practice, however, experience of open financial markets has not always been quite as positive as in theory. The suffering endured by Tiger Cubs and Asian Tigers (Indonesia, Malaysia, the Philippines, Thailand and South Korea) during the Asian crisis of 1997–1998 is representative of the downside of open financial markets. At that time, macroeconomic deficiencies such as external imbalances, high external, often USD-denominated debt coupled with insufficient reserve assets, but also inadequate financial supervision, caused foreign investors to lose confidence in large swathes of the region. They quickly and massively withdrew their funds, which had in many cases been invested for short-term speculative purposes. The result was a sharp drop in economic activity and a considerable surge in unemployment in the affected countries.

China, on the other hand, was relatively immune to the direct impact of the Asian crisis, given its lower external debt, lower budget deficit and in particular its higher stocks of reserve assets compared to the most affected countries. Many countries, including China, learned from the later that building up a high stock of reserve assets can be an effective protective shield. A more decisive factor for the much smaller impact of the Asian crisis on China, however, is likely to have been the fact that its financial account was much less open than that of its neighbours in the region at that time.

What the Asian crisis appears to have shown is that, in a setting of open financial markets, access to foreign capital could be assured if monetary policy is oriented to stability and an effective financial oversight regime is in place. If, however, poorly regulated short-term lending from abroad leads to a situation in which financial institutions can use excessive short-term funding to finance long-term assets, this would create illiquidity risks on balance sheets. Sudden capital flight could then quickly overwhelm and destabilise the entire domestic financial system. Moreover, borrowing in foreign currency which is not hedged against exchange rate risks harbours additional potential for destabilisation. A sharp currency depreciation would drive up the debt burden dramatically, force borrowers into insolvency and impede further funding from abroad, creating a vicious circle.

Renminbi's Reserve Status a Strong Motivation for Further Financial Market Opening

Seen in this context, the Asian crisis gave China good reason to tread carefully when opening up its financial markets. The salient feature of its journey so far has been a prudent and the process of lifting of its capital controls was gradually albeit not in straight line. Investor programmes for individual market segments with limited and rising investment ratios have been designed to ensure that China retains control of cross-border capital flows. As for opening itself up to investor groups, China again took a gradual approach, with a distinct preference for long-term investors.

However, the liberalisation process has not always gone smoothly. For instance, China fought a bout of downward pressure on the renminbi which persisted since the summer of 2015 by using considerable reserve assets and restrictions on capital outflows. Effective though these measures were in the short term, one may wonder why China now wants to push ahead even more quickly with efforts to open its financial markets and why the topic is high up the political agenda, despite the aforementioned risks and problems. To approach the answer, it pays to look at some key figures which are important for the country's self-image. China accounts for 18% of the world's aggregate GDP. It is the world's leader in merchandise exports, with a share of 13%, and is the number 2 merchandise importer at 11%. In the financial sector, China likewise occupies many of the top spots—even if the different stages of developments make it more difficult to compare cross-national. Its domestic bond market has the third-largest stock of outstanding bonds, behind Japan (number 2) and the United States (number 1), and the Chinese banking system is the world leader in terms of total assets, ahead of the euro area and the USA. In these categories, then, China has been in Champions League territory for quite some time already, and often with the prospect of having a lock on the title.

But there is another category, one that is important for China's self-perception, where it is currently still far removed from such echelons: its currency's status as a reserve currency. In 2016, the renminbi was included into the exclusive group of the now five key currencies which form the basis for the special drawing rights (SDRs) of the International Monetary Fund (IMF). Celebrated as a "historical milestone", the practical impact, however, has been, to put it charitably, modest, as China's currency accounts for a mere 1.8% of allocated global reserve assets. That is little more than the Australian dollar (1%) and less than the Canadian dollar (2%), neither of which is contained in the SDR basket, and virtually negligible compared to the share of the world's leading reserve currencies, the US dollar (62%) and the euro (20%).

But it is precisely the title of leading reserve currency which is arguably the most coveted accolade. Back in the 1960s, Valéry Giscard d'Estaing, then France's finance minister, said that the US dollar's status as the key currency in the Bretton Woods regime was an "exorbitant privilege" for the United States. But this status of a key currency still stands to this day, as the United States continues to enjoy relatively low interest rates because the government debt issued in its own currency is regarded as extremely safe, and is therefore sought after and held globally by reserve investors such as central banks and sovereign funds. This, for its part, generates additional downward pressure on yields and, according to conventional wisdom, helps the USA to fund both its foreign trade deficit and also its new borrowing less expensively than other countries.

The US dollar's status as a reserve currency is, moreover, associated with a certain shock absorbency capacity, since, in a crisis, investors will choose this currency as a safe haven for their investments in the absence of liquid alternatives—and thereby stabilise the US financial markets, though at the cost of an appreciating currency. For the domestic banking system, this is just as much of an advantage as the lower relative costs of hedging foreign currency exposures, given the global proliferation of the US dollar in the markets as a transaction currency. The money creation gains generated by the difference between the costs of printing money and its face value (seigniorage) are also considerable. The often large quantities of cash denominated in a reserve currency which are in circulation abroad make this seigniorage that much higher.

Against this background, from the Chinese point of view there seem to be particular benefits to the privilege of reserve currency status, which would outweigh the imponderables and problems of opening its financial markets. High global demand for the renminbi would significantly bolster and even expand China's stature on the world stage once it was able to capitalise in full on the advantages of bona fide reserve currency status.

However, reserve status would appear to be beyond reach without open financial markets. The economic history books, at least, tell us that even the USA was first and foremost an economic and trade powerhouse to begin with at the start of the past century, much as China is today. It wasn't until the mid-1920s that the US dollar achieved supremacy over its main competitor at the time, the pound sterling. The literature credits the more highly developed, deeper US financial markets with being the decisive factor.

Outlook

Story of Opening Up China's Financial Markets to Be Continued

So if China wishes to model its trajectory on the historical example of the US dollar, it will have to press ahead more vigorously and decisively than before with its current policy of gradual opening its financial markets. This more lasting desire to liberalise its financial markets might also be the essence of the new era President Xi referred to. For the story of China's opening-up is not really new. It already began under Deng Xiaoping in the late 1970s but, since then, has progressed more in waves, sometimes with large gaps or even setbacks in-between.

Another relevant factor is that the actual proclaimed concept for opening-up relates to "socialism with Chinese characteristics" marking a new chapter in China's rejuvenation. It would therefore be inaccurate to equate the opening of Chinese financial markets with a move towards Western-style democracy. Rather, these efforts towards liberalisation are—besides exploiting the general economic advantages—far more about eliminating once and for all the discrepancy between China's status as a real economic superpower and the marginal status of its currency as a reserve currency in the financial markets.

According to market participants, the outlook for this is encouraging, notably, as central banks are well-known slow movers with regards to new markets. According to a survey conducted by HSBC for 2018, global reserve managers expect the share of the renminbi as a global reserve currency to increase to 8.5% by 2020 and 15% by 2030.

If we expand our view, we see another project, one that is actually directed entirely elsewhere, as being complementary to China's monetary interests: the Belt and Road Initiative (BRI), also known as "new Silk Road". This flagship project which China is dynamically pursuing is intended, in future, to create the infrastructure for several routes along which trade with Europe will be intensified. Chinese banks are eagerly providing funding for this project in renminbi. This means that the Belt and Road Initiative would not only have a real economic effect of intensifying trade but could also jump-start demand for renminbi among borrowers based in countries located along these new trade routes. Those countries, however, would have to keep a watch on the sustainability of their debts denominated in foreign currencies.

Finally, a factor which will be of particular importance from a central bank perspective is how China treats one element which has always been seen as a decisive precondition for a leading reserve currency to reap its dividends: the confidence of global investors. Only if they have faith in the renminbi as an asset which is readily available, stable in value, and can be redeemed in goods and services without major frictions will its status as a leading reserve currency be cemented in the long term. For this to happen, will it be necessary to adapt additional properties of current reserve currencies? Will China introduce more elements of the rule of law? Will China be able to continue the stability-oriented economic, fiscal and monetary policy—well aware of the in traditional textbooks described trilemma between free capital movement, fixed exchange rate and independent central bank? Or will there ultimately be another way, one with Chinese characteristics? The jury is still out.

CHAPTER 7

Simple Rules for a Complex Relationship

Jörg Wuttke

Why Is China Going Global?

For Chinese companies, internationalisation is the most practical way to buy Western know-how. The wish lists of the companies range from patents and technologies to management, process, system and strategic expertise. However, entering the markets of industrial countries also requires internationally known brands and global production and distribution networks. And here, most Chinese companies are only beginning to get organised. Many acquisitions and partnerships thus primarily serve as a strategy to gain brand rights as well as useful sales, marketing and service structure. Chinese companies are also eager to move into the European Union (EU) markets, as they are less cutthroat. It's harder to turn a profit in China for a number of reasons, including a lack of protection for intellectual property, which means knock-off products are created quickly and profits are hard to maintain. As customers are so price sensitive, and margins are so razor thin, Chinese companies often lack the resources to make sustained investments in research and development. Top Chinese companies derive their impetus for overseas expansion from internal corporate

J. Wuttke (✉)
European Union Chamber of Commerce in China, Beijing, China

T. Wenniges, W. Lohman (eds.), *Chinese FDI in the EU and the US*,
https://doi.org/10.1007/978-981-13-6071-8_7

dynamics (need for raw materials, supply improvements, acquire complementary technology, etc.).

The market penetration of Chinese companies in industrial countries is often complicated and difficult. The companies often still lack a clear focus on a specific segment in which a core competence and a strong brand name are to be established. In view of the strong competitive pressures in China, only a very few companies are able to build up the financial reserves needed for financing the step-by-step expansion of foreign business locations. Moreover, not all Chinese competitive advantages can be transferred to other markets and consumer habits. The Chinese often lack experience in international marketing and an effective logistics and service structure. Foreign legal systems cause difficulties for them—particularly the corporate, environmental and labour laws in Europe. Chinese companies frequently snap up bankrupt EU companies for minimal outlays without previously conducting a thorough analysis of all the associated problems. Often their strategic concept is based on nothing more than the vague idea to 'combine Western technology with Chinese costs'.

China's global outward foreign direct investment (FDI) has been on an impressive growth trajectory for the past decade, with an annual average growth rate of 30 per cent from 2005 to 2019. In 2016, Chinese outbound investment grew faster than this historical rate, in part driven by the desire of corporations to diversify in the face of a slowing domestic economy, financial stress and devaluation pressure on the Chinese currency, with estimates that Chinese outward FDI came close to USD 200 billion in 2016, a 40 per cent increase from 2015 levels. This cements China's role as one of the top direct investor nations globally.

The Chinese authorities have also started guiding state-sponsored investment of Chinese companies abroad, with much of it flowing into high-tech industries covered by the 'Made in China 2025' (CM2025) initiative. China's global outbound foreign direct investment (OFDI) jumped to almost USD 200 billion in 2016, an increase so great that Chinese policymakers started to slow down the pace of outbound investment expansion in late 2016. The EU continues to be a favourite destination for Chinese investors, with more than EUR 30 billion of completed OFDI transactions in 2017. This stands in contrast with a further drop in investment by European firms in China in the same year.

Why Is the EU So Interesting to Chinese Investors?

The European Union (EU) is viewed by Chinese investors as a safe, stable destination for investment. It has the largest global well-off consumer market for sales of goods and services, as well as advanced technologies, an educated workforce and desirable brands. Chinese companies are still mostly looking to access the European market to sell their goods and services, while an increasing number are looking to acquire technologies, expertise and brands through mergers and acquisitions (M&A) with European companies to improve their capacity to compete both in China and abroad.

In light of the challenges faced by China's economy, like overcapacity in many products, it is unsurprising that Chinese companies have looked to diversify their asset base into Europe's open economy. As China now accounts for 14 per cent of global gross domestic product (GDP), it can be expected to continue to become an increasingly important source of international investment. Europe greatly welcomes foreign investment from China and around the globe. It actively works to attract this investment for the jobs, economic growth and international business connections that it creates. The attractiveness of the largest economic region in the world—the EU—is enhanced by the fact that foreign investors enjoy the same legal protections that are enjoyed by their domestic counterparts. Nor has the EU established a review body to evaluate transactions that could result in foreign individuals or entities gaining control of EU-based companies. In addition, the EU is regarded as an open market, with fewer market access barriers than the US and little history of opposition to Chinese investments on national security grounds. It is an open and attractive destination for Chinese investment.

How Does the Chinese Government Steer OFDI?

Chinese enterprises report that government OFDI encouragement policies are largely viewed to be of assistance to state-owned enterprises (SOEs) only, with private enterprises getting little help. China's 'national champions' receive cheap land and finance, tax breaks and preferential access to listing their shares. By operating in previously protected markets, large state-owned enterprises have accumulated cash hoards that they can use to buy assets abroad. China started to streamline the outbound investment approval processes also to prevent capital flights, and it enhanced the on-the-ground support in Europe and established a chamber of commerce for Chinese enterprises in some EU member states like Germany.

The European Union Chamber of Commerce in China holds concerns that the priority sectors outlined in the Chinese government's innovation blueprint CM2025 (China Manufacturing 2025) amount to a 'shopping list' of companies and technologies in the EU that China has not been able to develop domestically. As 70 per cent of the Chinese investment that flowed into Europe in 2015 came from SOEs, it is likely no coincidence that many of these investments have been in industries like advanced machinery, robotics, semiconductors and clean technology—all priorities for China under CM2025. A study released by the Bertelsmann Foundation in May 2018, ahead of a trip by the German Chancellor Angela Merkel to China, showed that 64 per cent of Chinese investments in Germany over the past three years were in sectors Beijing is prioritising as part of its CM2025 strategy.

Structural Parameters Have to Be Resolved on Both Sides

The EU should maintain its openness for foreign investment and continue to encourage outbound direct investment from China. China should look to develop various aspects of its international relations for the benefit of Chinese enterprises going overseas through means such as opening up the domestic market to European firms and, in particular, remedying situations where Chinese companies can invest in certain European sectors, when the reverse is not possible. This should nullify this issue as an irritant and lessen the chance of greater opposition to Chinese investment as a retaliatory measure in return. This gap in market access is as significant as it is unsustainable. In the past, China's status as a developing economy rendered reciprocity much less of an issue. This has now changed. As a USD 10 trillion economy—the world's second largest, China is now far more important than it was ten or even five years ago. This is reflected in the fact that from 2010 to 2015, China's total OFDI tripled. As Premier Li has stated that during the period 2016 to 2020 China may deploy USD 1 trillion of capital abroad, this figure may shortly double again.

As China's largest trading partner, the EU represents about 15 per cent of the country's trade. Since it is also a leading destination for its outbound investment, China needs the EU possibly more than the EU needs

China. The question of whether China will be willing to offer reciprocity therefore has serious ramifications, both for European business today and for how in the longer term Chinese investments will be perceived internationally. If it is ultimately unwilling to offer reciprocal access to its own market, China cannot assume that it will indefinitely continue to enjoy open and unhindered access to the EU market. The liberal approach to M&A will only work if all parties move towards equal access and the removal of barriers; otherwise, it is politically untenable.

As the June 2016 European Commission paper 'Elements for a New EU Strategy on China' puts it: 'The EU welcomes productive Chinese investment in Europe provided it is in line with EU law and regulations. In return, the EU expects improved market access for foreign companies in China and a level playing field for business and investments. China should reduce the number of protected sectors and minimize national security reviews'. German Chancellor Angela Merkel echoed this sentiment during her trip to China in May 2018, in her comments on Chinese companies' high level of interest in acquiring German businesses. 'If we are open', she said, 'it must be possible to find good solutions here too. We do, of course, expect reciprocity from the Chinese side'.

In the reform programme propagated by the Chinese Communist Party in November 2013—the Decision—the Chinese government pledged to remove a wide range of market access barriers. Unfortunately, since evaluating China's reform progress in the Position Paper 2015/2016, the European Union Chamber of Commerce in China has noted only limited improvement. On 10 July 2018 the Chamber issued a report, '18 Months Since Davos: How China's Vision Became a Reform Imperative', http://www.europeanchamber.com.cn/en/publications-18-months-since-davos. The report covers the reform promises by President Xi Jinping at the World Economic Forum in Davos in 2017, where Xi asserted that China would step up to take a leading role in the global economic system and further open up to international business. The chamber comes to the conclusion that '[w]hile the pace of reform has accelerated, compared to the demands of the rapidly developing Chinese economy, China's reforms are, in absolute terms, still insufficient and incomplete'. This inertia to fulfil public commitments granting reciprocal access for investment is increasingly detrimental to the Chinese authorities' ability to achieve their own goals. A prolonged dip in FDI into China, which may have already begun with European investment in China declining during the last four years in a row, would indicate a loss of interest among foreign investors.

This could lead to a further decline in confidence over the country's ability to maintain long-term economic growth and would in no way support the Chinese government's ongoing efforts to foster new drivers of economic growth.

It is therefore an increasingly serious concern that reciprocal market access has yet to be extended to European business in China. In contrast to Chinese companies who face few, if any, limitations in investing in European industries like construction, financial services, healthcare, insurance, logistics, media and telecommunications, European companies in China continue to either be fully barred from participation or limited to holding a minority position. The Market Access Negative List on domestic and international investment that was released in March 2016 indicates that minimal progress has been made in opening up the market to more competition. While it is too soon to draw a definitive conclusion, the draft revisions that were announced for the Foreign Investment Catalogue in December 2017 include many significant changes. As a result, while the complementarities of pairing Europe's technology, know-how and capital with China's supply chain, market and capital are attractive, in many industries, European companies' only options for accessing the Chinese market are to license their technology, take on a Chinese investor or be fully acquired.

However, China's singular success possesses within itself the seeds that can undo the contemporary model of globalisation. Two recent examples follow below. In 2016, leaders from Europe scrutinised more incoming Chinese companies' products and investments. The increase in dumping cases being brought against China in the steel, paper and chemicals sectors indicates a need to protect jobs and industries against the perceived trade juggernaut that is China. In early 2016, 5000 EU steel workers also took to the streets of Brussels to protest the closure of their plants, in part as a result of overcapacity in China's impact on the industry. This marked the first demonstration ever held in Europe against trade relations with the country, with calls from member states and industry groups also made for further anti-dumping measures.

In view of rising populism in Europe, the mood towards trade and investment relations with China are shifting. In a May 2016 non-legislative resolution the European Parliament resolved that until China has fulfilled the EU's five criteria for market economy status (MES), its exports to the EU must be treated in a 'non-standard' way. This resolution was subsequently passed by Members of the European Parliament

(MEPs). A consensus was formed that the EU 'should assess whether China's costs and prices are market-based, so as to ensure a level playing field for EU industry and defend EU jobs'. The European Parliament also stressed that the EU must find a way to do this in compliance with its international obligations in the World Trade Organization (WTO), and in particular China's WTO Accession Protocol, which provided for changes to how China is to be treated in trade cases after the 15th anniversary of its accession on 11 December 2016.

In May 2018 MEPs voted on a proposal that will broaden the powers of the European Commission to scrutinise foreign investments amid rising concern about Chinese acquisitions on the continent. The international trade committee of the parliament has been debating roughly 450 amendments to a legislative proposal presented by the Commission in 2017. The parliament's proposal was stronger than that of the Commission's in several respects: it did extend the list of sectors that could draw EU scrutiny and oblige the EU executive to vet suspect investments, rather than just giving it the option to do so. The draft gives a far wider definition of critical infrastructure and technologies that could trigger the screening process. Among the sectors added to the list include the media, ports, the automotive sector and election infrastructure. The Commission's proposal states that the EU executive 'may screen' foreign direct investments that are likely to affect projects or programmes of Union interest on the grounds of security or public order. The parliament's version hardens the language to 'shall screen'. While the proposed legislation would give the Commission the right to issue opinions and collect investment information from member states, it would leave the final say on whether to block foreign investments to national authorities.

What Do Chinese Companies in EU Encounter?

Operating in the EU, however, is not perceived as easy and there are numerous obstacles often relating to bureaucratic procedures and high costs. Key obstacles relate to obtaining visas and work permits for Chinese employees, dealing with European labour laws, human resources (HR) costs and cultural differences in management style. Understanding various operating regulations such as tax laws is an issue, as these are complex due to the lack of uniform legislation across the 28 EU member states and the reality of 23 different EU languages.

European policymakers with responsibility for inbound investment should examine what can be done to better encourage future investment, including:

- look to address the operational issues relating to bureaucracy and cost;
- look to offer practical solutions to minimise the complexities of a market of 27 separate legal and tax regimes as well as 23 languages, such as establishing a source of consolidated legal information for all EU member states in one language;
- investigate the reported obstacles in the FDI approval processes and see if these can be streamlined; and
- better communicate the openness of the EU market due to the reported lack of awareness amongst potential Chinese investors.

Chinese companies going global have to get to grips with very different management styles, cultures, priorities and mindsets. Cultural issues can be a hurdle. In addition to the issues that face any company looking to expand inorganically (such as post-integration planning, adapting to new business environments and balancing short- and long-term value creation), Chinese companies face the hurdle of getting to grips with very different management styles, culture, priorities and mindsets of other companies. Of the Chinese joint venture failures, the majority of CEOs attributed their difficulties to differences in managerial styles and corporate culture. Chinese managers have to conform to international standards, systems and processes. Their corporate governance framework in particular remains underdeveloped, as proven in the recent ZTE debacle.

Chinese companies still often lack managerial expertise and experience, and face obstacles in the war for talent. European multinationals still enjoy advantages in terms of pay and prestige. Cultivation of international management and staff is after all the transnational companies' no. 1 success factor. Chinese companies lack flexible salary and hiring practices and rotate their talents too fast in their overseas assignments. Lack of local language skills and cultural affinity could be resolved by the ever-increasing diaspora of Chinese talent—Western educated and familiar with Chinese culture and values—who does provide a valuable resource for Chinese companies going global. Another trademark of Chinese companies operating in the EU is that virtually none has an internationally staffed advisory board.

Foreign Investment Flops Are the Result of Such Strategic Miscalculations

Chinese investments abroad often used to be unsuccessful. In Germany, the most prominent case is that of TCL, which bought troubled German TV manufacturer Schneider in 2002 and the television business of Thompson in 2003. TCL's mobile phone joint venture with France's Alcatel also didn't live up to expectations and was ended early in the summer of 2005, only eight months after being launched. Another example is the bankruptcy of China's D'Long, which had unsuccessfully dabbled in everything from oranges, noodles, cement and lawn mowers to the German plane manufacturer Fairchild Dornier. D'Long, once one of China's biggest private companies, failed in part due to its murky financing channels.

For a while, the bankruptcy of Chinese companies abroad threatened to ruin the good reputation of Chinese firms as solid entrepreneurs. To counteract this negative image, the Chinese government established guidelines in 2004 for company acquisitions abroad. These are intended to help Chinese firms better select acquisition candidates, more realistically evaluate the hurdles of foreign labour and corporate laws, and pursue their objectives with greater strategic skills. In addition, Chinese companies are now more frequently drawing on the support of large Western law firms, consulting companies and lobbying offices in their acquisitions and takeover attempts.

CHAPTER 8

One Voice of Europe?

Diego Andreis

Introduction

EU Needs to Speak and Act as One to Shape Future-Proof Trade Agreements

Comparison of main parameters between EU and China

Issue	*European Union*	*People's Republic of China*
Trade (goods—import)[a]	€374.8 billion	€198.2 billion
Trade (services—import)[b]	€29.6 billion	€38.3 billion
R&D[c]	€301.8 billion	€155.4 billion

[a]Eurostat figures: http://ec.europa.eu/trade/policy/countries-and-regions/countries/china/
[b]Eurostat figures: http://ec.europa.eu/trade/policy/countries-and-regions/countries/china/
[c]Eurostat figures and Ceemet calculations: https://ec.europa.eu/eurostat/statistics-explained/index.php/R_%26_D_expenditure

D. Andreis (✉)
Ceemet – European Tech and Industry Employers, Milan, Italy
e-mail: combuechen@ceemet.org

T. Wenniges, W. Lohman (eds.), *Chinese FDI in the EU and the US*,
https://doi.org/10.1007/978-981-13-6071-8_8

The European Union

The European project has led to over 60 years of peace and the creation of wealth on the European continent, though these facts are often overlooked in particular by some of its younger citizens. There is now a generation which has grown up around this idea of peace in Europe and anything else seems foreign to them. These achievements would not have been possible without a fair degree of unity among the European Union (EU)'s member states, which has become more challenging and needed some calibration after the historic enlargement of the European Union in 2004. Today, this unity is being challenged by issues such as Brexit and the election of populists across the continent. This has led to increasing scepticism towards the European project's ability to cope with globalisation and fast technological change, recent economic crisis and the ongoing migration crisis. However, the roots of the EU run deep, and its single market continues to deliver wealth and prosperity to its member states, their citizens, companies and workers.

The EU creates wealth not only with its inward-looking single market of well above 500 million people, but also with its outward-looking trade policy and free trade agreements with large economies such as Canada or Japan, which, once approved by the Council, will be sent for approval to the European Parliament. Only with the combined clout of that level of the gross domestic product (GDP) is the EU in such a position to negotiate positive terms for its companies to trade under.

Globalisation

It is common knowledge that China is a very important market and trading partner for the EU. International trade (and as a characteristic of that, global value chains) has positive effects on wealth creation and is a driver of innovation, for example, by using the advantages of the specialisation in particular countries that are involved in a global value chain.

The EU and China are two of the biggest trade powers in the world. While China is the EU's second biggest trading partner, with the US still being number one, the EU is China's biggest trading partner, with the EU having a trade deficit with China. This goes some way towards explaining why the latest Commission report on Trade and Investment Barriers of June 2018 placed China among the top-ranked countries when it comes to trade and investment barriers, with the largest increase in new barriers in 2017, the Information and Communications Technology (ICT) and electronic sector have the highest barriers.

With the current nervousness surrounding globalisation and digitalisation and being aware of some fundamental differences in the political and economic systems, the EU and China have the responsibility and the opportunity to write a new chapter of their trade relations that could become the standard of the twenty-first century. As any other agreement, to be sustainable, this needs to be done within a partnership of equals.

During recent years, the EU's relationship with China has been mostly characterised by policies and initiatives of individual EU member states rather than being shaped by a common policy of the European Union. One of the obvious assets of the European Union is that it is the largest economy and trading bloc in the world. This massive potential too often is not leveraged to its full and too often only for short-term national and political interests. The member states of the EU should focus on the bigger picture and the common denominators and potential threats of an uncoordinated approach, showing that international trade has created wealth, driven innovation and competitiveness and contributed to top-level social spending in Europe.

All stakeholders, in the first instance politicians, but also companies, workers and European citizens, should understand the upsides of a common European trade policy and its implementation, provided it is to promote a fair trade around the world, such as is in the example of EU-Canada Comprehensive Economic and Trade Agreement (CETA), where workers' rights have been guaranteed in Europe.

The example of a national or regional government, challenging the result achieved through yearlong negotiations between Canada and the European Commission, based on a Council mandate that had been made public, seems to be a logical consequence of the current trend of nationalism and protectionism. The explanation of that current trend has no doubt many aspects, one of which might well be that the European Commission has, despite many efforts, not managed to find the right way of communicating with its citizens and the business. Instead of approaching each other, the EU and its citizens have become more and more alienated over the years, when reassurance that Europe can offer an answer to globalisation and digitalisation is so much needed. Continuing to go down that route, in my view, will favour neither European citizens, nor European business and their workers. Yet, there are signs of confidence, as, against all these odds, CETA—as one of the most comprehensive and advanced international trade deals—has eventually been signed.

Europe's companies and citizens have a vested interest in reasonably transparent negotiating processes, which, in line with European standards, are democratically accountable. Shaping the relations with China requires equal partners in order to broker an agreement that ensures a level-playing field. It would be an important move of the People's Republic of China to better accommodate these principles of transparency and accountability, leading to a balanced EU-China relation, as we can see from the recent Transatlantic Trade and Investment Partnership (TTIP) negotiations—the EU has become much more transparent and it is up to our trade partners to do the same.

Investment

China's engagements in Europe have increased and translated into investments in European infrastructures and strategically important companies, representing the DNA of Europe's unparalleled industrial tissue. On the other hand, the EU is not in a position to invest on the same terms and conditions in China. This must be addressed in any investment agreement. Both sides shall offer predictable, long-term and reciprocal access to each other's markets and ensure the protection of investors and their investments. Given the speed and magnitude of Chinese investments, often supported by loans from state banks, the initiative of the Ministers of Economy from Italy, France and Germany in early 2017 has made the Commission present a proposal on more stringent investment screenings. However, the EU again seems to be undermining its possibility to speak with one voice, which does not go unnoticed by our trading partners, including China.

In the long run, balanced agreements would be accepted by the general public in Europe and by definition be more sustainable. Whatever the position is about screening of investment, it has to strike a balance and not unduly hamper investments. The Commission's suggestion of a European-level coordination of countries which has put in place such screening, to me, is a reasonable and important first step. Single countries' checks on foreign direct investment (FDI) are often not enough, because as single countries, there can often be a lack of an understanding of the broader picture and member states could be tempted to take the short-term approach for short-term gains, which may have been considered as a way to mitigate a difficult economic situation. Furthermore, it is only logical that it is easier for a disproportionately larger economic power to negotiate preferential agreements with single European member states than with a united cluster of 28 or 27 EU member states. For Europe, another challenge will be to raise awareness and work with all European countries where screening is not in place to put such systems in place, ensuring they don't become a point of entry for sensitive FDI, as this would eventually undermine the joint efforts of the other EU member states. Sharing a framework and executing a coordinated FDI screening at European level would not do harm to national interests; on the contrary, it would be in line with the principle of subsidiarity.

Industrial Policy

An Industrial Policy for an Internationally Competitive Industry in Europe

In 2013, China presented its "Made in China 2025" plan, an adaptation of the "Strategic Emerging Industries" plan of 2006. The objective of the initiative is to comprehensively upgrade Chinese industry and to move the country's manufacturing up the value chain and gain technological leadership. The difference from the previous plan is that "Made in China 2025" is focusing not just on the development of innovation and advanced technologies, but on the entire value chain.

The "EU-China 2020 Strategic Agenda for Cooperation" was launched also in 2013. The European Commission understood that it needed an own strategy which puts the EU's interests at the forefront in the EU-China relationship. In a first step it published a European Commission communication in 2016 which was interpreted as a response to the "Made in China 2025" plan, resulting in a "New Industrial Policy Strategy" presented by Commission President Jean-Claude Juncker in his State of the European Union in September 2017 (Commission Communication on Industrial Renaissance, 2014). The objective of the strategy was to provide the right framework conditions to make European industries stay ahead in innovation, digitisation and decarbonisation, though I would have expected this New Strategy to be more ambitious and, particularly, its execution plan to be more effective. We all hope that the necessary silver bullet for an internationally competitive industry in Europe will be swiftly devised by the recently set up High Level Industrial Round Table "Industry 2030".

Recently the Commission also came up with several communications and initiatives on digitising European industry. From my perception as CEO of an internationally linked and active enterprise, with the home base being in Italy, this is much appreciated to be organised in an efficient way and implemented in the field. Small- and medium-sized companies across Europe need much more than just high-level initiatives from Europe, which are rarely felt in the real world, to be able to thrive through this digital era. This need is even stronger in the EU-13 and Southern regions, which need support to make the massive investments that are necessary to provide the digital infrastructure and educate and train people to be fit for the digital era. I am convinced that also in the area of digitalisation, individual nation-states cannot successfully compete with the big economic and fast-moving regions in the world. Overall, the successful digital transition of societies and industry in Europe is a genuinely European issue, holding the potential of writing a new chapter of the success story of our European project.

However, Europe must go further and develop its own "Made in Europe" equivalent. Any (common) position and strategy in trade, investment, and industrial policy must ensure a level-playing field between the EU and China. Furthermore, the Commission itself should better streamline its work practices and improve communication between its various directorates in order to maximise the trade relationships it creates.

From my experience as an entrepreneur, having invested in China for more than 15 years, I have always been impressed by the ability of China to not only plan, but execute accordingly, and their "Made in China 2025" looks like it will confirm this. The fact that the EU is operating in a different political environment cannot continue to be an excuse for not implementing the strategies and reaching the targets, for example, the European Commission target that by 2020, the contribution of industry to GDP in Europe should reach 20%. If there is agreement, which I think exists, that industry is part of the solution to the societal, economic and ecological challenges, then the EU, that is, its national heads of states and governments, must not only speak with one voice, but also back up what they are saying.

Digitalisation Goes Beyond National Borders

Digitalisation is cutting through all aspects of our social and economic lives, including trade relations, creating new opportunities and challenges. Digitalisation is the new normal and will no doubt become more and more pervasive in our future. Digitalisation should therefore be the basis for adapting the trade relationship between the EU and China.

With exponential developments in digitalisation, we currently see a new wave of globalisation in services. Whereas overall trade in goods has gone down since 2014 (WTO), traffic of and trade in "data" have gone up tremendously over the past 30 years. The monthly volume of global data traffic increased from 0.001 petabyte in 1990 to 20,151 petabytes in 2010 to 109,000 petabytes in 2017 (Statista, Cisco). A precondition for Europe to be an equal partner in that new form of trade relationship is the swift completion of a seamless Digital Single Market[1,2] Standards, the common technical rules that allow data communications, should be set on a common basis and not be the monopoly of a few, to allow seamless and secure access to people and companies around the globe.

Digitalisation and artificial intelligence will continue to develop exponentially and push the reality beyond humans' linear imagination. National borders already have and will continue to become less important in trading between economies, companies and people. Digitalisation will force governments around the world to find new approaches to trading.

People are at the heart of the fourth industrial revolution, more so than during the previous three industrial revolutions. Europe must invest, nurture and grow the skills of its citizens. Europe's main trading proposition will be more and more generated by the quality of brains of its people, its entrepreneurs, engineers, workers and the ecosystem around them, and so forth.

Trade

International Trade

The European Union is one of the world powerhouses of trade and a first mover on globalisation. However, to ensure the continuation of this trade, it must be based on international rules, standards and norms, with fair competition between all actors. Free trade and open markets have been key drivers of the prosperity which we enjoy in the EU. In a challenging global environment of increased nationalism and protectionism, the EU must continue striving for new types of international trade agreements,

[1] COM(2015) 192 of 6 May 2015, Communication on "A Digital Single Market Strategy for Europe".

[2] https://ec.europa.eu/digital-single-market/en/news/completing-trusted-digital-single-market-all.

while protecting our existing trade relations. However, these trade agreements must address global risks, from overproduction to intellectual property rights (IPR), and ensure investment from both sides, while not lowering European social standards.

Free and fair trade is a source of wealth in the European Union. We must jointly defend European interests not only in global trade, but also against the sea change in the transatlantic partnership. This sea change can be shown by the recent 10% tariff placed on aluminium and 25% tariff on steel exports from the EU to the US. These tariffs will see damage done not only to the EU metals sector, but also the US economy as a whole. Furthermore, the US is now out of the Paris climate agreement, and its interest in the WTO, being aware of the need for its reform, seems to be waning.

Globalisation is one of the biggest phenomena of our time; it has been hugely important for wealth creation and is the backbone of the social systems which we have developed in Europe. These social models have been built on the wealth generated by globalisation, which shall continue to provide growth, prosperity and jobs within Western and developed economies. Global value chains have led to small- and medium-sized enterprises being able to take part in the global economy, and in this highly integrated global economy, they will continue to foster competition and innovation.

Belt and Road Initiative (BRI)

The Belt and Road Initiative (BRI) project, which so far can be seen as a one-way (Chinese) project, both in the planning and in the execution, should also bring a sense of urgency for an EU approach in this area. For China, the initiative is of such importance that it is has been included in the Chinese Communist Party programme at the end of 2017. Given this, China has to build trust when carrying out this initiative.

BRI must be transparent and ensure a level-playing field based on market rules and international norms, and there must be complementarity and reciprocity between the EU's and China's policies and projects. The EU-China Connectivity Platform is a good way to establish cooperation, including on rail links, working together with TEN-T projects to link the already existing cohesion and interconnection of the trans-European transport network to that of the BRI. In today's world sustainable trade agreements can only be reached if there is parity between the different parties involved. The EU and China should realise quickly that in the end, the power of digitalisation is bigger than their political and economic power, and that the window of opportunity to broker fair and balanced free trade deals will close faster than they will imagine.

What we now see is surging opposition to the BRI, as there are counter-initiatives from other regions across the world, such as India and Japan, which ideally should not run counter to the goals of free trade. It seems obvious that this fragmented and polarised approach is not the blueprint of a twenty-first-century international trade deal. With a lack of transparency and trust, the BRI even risks creating a divide between EU member states. This must be avoided, again, by devising a single European position to seize the benefits from global trade, which entails that China too must further open its market. Europe also cannot ignore the shift in the transatlantic partnership. Therefore, Europe should strike more partnerships with other blocs and economic powers in the world and has to cooperate on the BRI and defend its goals, which include free and fair trade and avoiding a downward spiral of European (social) standards. The EU has urged China to set rules on transparency, debt sustainability, open procurement processes and the environment at the heart of the BRI. These terms and conditions have to be clearly spelled out and fixed in an agreement.

Foreign Direct Investment

While a balanced and reciprocal FDI has a positive effect on all economies, this must be carried out in a long-term and sustainable way. It is very easy for member states of the EU to make decisions based on a short-term view, particularly during crisis cycles. This can make countries focus on short-term value, while missing out the long-term impact of such choices. The EU should serve to put together the broader picture and analyse the FDI with a long-term view as well as with a European view.

This is particularly true when the parties involved have very different economical resources, as in the case of China and member states of the EU. The investments which China makes are often said to have a long-term view, not least due to their one-party system. China lately has completed large investments in the EU, not least through KUKA, the German robotic group, just to mention one of the most prominent examples, and the Greek port of Piraeus, which is one of the European flagship initiatives of China's BRI.

China is massively attracting inward investment and spending heavily on the purchasing of EU companies. Because of lower barriers in Europe versus the US, in the first half of 2018, total Chinese investments in the US and Canada reached only $2 billion, down 92% in the same period of last year, while Europe absorbed $12 billion in completed Chinese investments, six times the North American inflows. Furthermore, Europe received $20 billion in announced Chinese M&A debt against the $2.5 billion in M&A announced deals in North America in the same period.

Not to forget, particularly because of the financial crisis, some EU countries are still struggling and can be weak prey for easy money. Some of the European Union member states opened for foreign direct investments from China at conditions that can only provide short-term "solutions" as these countries find themselves in highly difficult economic situations (as an example, China bought strategic harbour of Piraeus as gateway into the EU for €281 million in 2016, resulting in Greece opposing the EU from taking a tougher stand on China's investment screening). As a direct result, the imbalance in development widened. One of the consequences of the crisis and this approach is the creation of a patchwork of different bilateral investment treaties between member states and China, which made finding a common position amongst the diverse types of relations and interests of the member states vis-à-vis China far more complicated.

Yet the opening-up of markets has to become a two-way street. In the meantime, state-owned enterprises are not only becoming multinational organisations but globally leading companies without respect for equal treatment of companies on the domestic market. It is a fair objective having an industry that is competitive on a global level, even though production is local and brand recognition is international, but trust can only be built over time and is based on a respectful execution of what has been agreed, with rules that apply to everyone.

There can be no doubt that intellectual property rights must be respected; this is particularly pertinent in times of digitalisation, where data is the new currency and with the increased level of cyberattacks on companies and public authorities. It is for this reason that the cybersecurity strategy of the European Commission has to be welcomed. Furthermore, a coordinated approach based on clear and simple rules must be promoted. This would help in the building of bilateral FDI discussions and execution between countries. This is particularly needed with China, which has always had a very clear and strong position on inbound FDI. China's recent signs of improving the conditions for inbound FDI should be encouraged and pursued.

Beside a well-written agreement, execution and verification should also be allowed and planned. In my experience I have seen and heard many times differences between what was said and what was done. We need to make sure that all parties involved do what they say and say what they do.

In relation to inward FDI in China, European companies must be treated the same as local companies, and this shall include state-owned companies as well. The issue of a forced knowledge transfer must be openly addressed and settled reasonably. While I believe there is much more value to be extracted from EU-China FDI compared to today, I also believe these shall be the result of a well-negotiated, bilateral agreement, which respects the long-term vision of both the EU and China. It should be built to be a sustainable win-win agreement.

By promoting reciprocity, a level-playing field and fair competition across all areas, a sound cooperation can be achieved which promotes universal values and recognises the importance of liability of contracts and trust.

Market Economy Status

In 2016, China requested that the country's WTO Accession Protocol, which expired that year, would enable the automatic granting of market economy status (MES). However, the EU, the US and other members of the WTO were cautious whether to implement the changes to the Accession Protocol. This would have weakened the anti-dumping instruments available to countries importing Chinese products. This complex legal debate was played out against the backdrop of geopolitical and commercial concerns, leading China, the US and the EU to take very different positions. There are many sides to this argument, but what can be agreed by all is that we must ensure free and fair global trade, based on clear rules and norms, and that market economy status can only be granted when these criteria are achieved.

Conclusions

From a Ceemet (European Tech and Industry Employers) point of view, the following conclusions and policy recommendations emerge:

- Free and fair trade are a source of wealth creation, innovation and overall prosperity.

- Digitalisation has kicked off new waves of globalisation. People and their skills are at the heart of this.
- Europe must devise its own commonly shared vision of a European silk road initiative of fair and free trade.
- A balanced, twenty-first-century trade deal between the EU and China as equal partners is a great opportunity for the two countries and must be found within a closing window of opportunity.
- The EU must, also in light of the advantages of global value chains, develop an own, more ambitious, industrial strategy and make sure to develop the right framework and deploy adequate resources for its execution. This should also feed into the Commission's high-level roundtable "Industry 2030".

These recommendations will also be upheld in the Ceemet 10 Point Plan for a competitive industry sustaining social Europe that will be launched at the end of September 2018 as the tech industries input in view of the preparation of the elections to the new European Parliament and the new European Commission in 2019.

CHAPTER 9

Rising to the Challenge: The EU and Chinese Strategic Investments in Europe

Roland Freudenstein

The Political Context

The year 2017 will be remembered as the year when China's growing global influence visibly turned from opportunity to challenge. This is due to concrete changes in substance and rhetoric on the Chinese side, as well as to a more attentive Western reaction to long-term developments in China itself, and in the West's economic and political relations with the People's Republic of China. The year represents a remarkable trajectory in European perceptions of the nature of China's influence and its potential character as an opportunity or a threat. At the beginning of 2017, U.S. President Donald Trump's inauguration speech, with its unbridled 'America First!' economic nationalism and disrespect for the Global Liberal Order, had sent shivers down the spines of many Europeans. In contrast to that, only a few days before, Chinese President Xi Jinping's 2017 Davos speech seemed to herald China as the new champion and defender of globalisation. Some in Europe began dreaming of a European

R. Freudenstein (✉)
Wilfried Martens Centre for European Studies, Brussels, Belgium
e-mail: rf@martenscentre.eu

T. Wenniges, W. Lohman (eds.), *Chinese FDI in the EU and the US*,
https://doi.org/10.1007/978-981-13-6071-8_9

Union (EU)-China alliance for trade and fighting climate change, and implicitly or explicitly against an America that seemed to turn inward.

And yet, only months later, this positive image of China lay in tatters. Concerning Europe, this was due mainly to three factors: First, in the summer of 2017, EU negotiators were shocked to see the Chinese government, or, more precisely, the Chinese Communist Party (CCP), let the EU-China summit go up in flames because the EU side insisted on linking the recognition of China's market economy status to concrete conditions (Godement and Vasselier 2017). Second, at the 19th CCP Congress in October 2017, President Xi spoke at length about a 'Chinese model' that would now be actively spread across the world. In order to do so, China would use a broad array of tools, ranging from a sustained military build-up to enhanced diplomacy, to reinforced efforts to spread propaganda, to utilising Chinese foreign direct investment (FDI). Although FDI naturally serves to create economic benefits, it has to be also defined as a tool to spread Chinese political influence. In the mindset of the CCP, these two goals are not mutually exclusive, but quite the contrary. Third, Chinese use of 'sharp power' as discussed in numerous publications in 2017–2018 has become a topic of policy debates in Europe and will become inseparable from the debate on Chinese FDI. Consequently, by the end of 2017, the stage was set for a much more critical appraisal of all of China's interactions with its partners.

The Challenge of Chinese FDI

It is in this context that the economic relations between the EU and China in general, and in mutual investment in particular, have to be analysed. Chinese FDI in the EU has rapidly increased in recent years. The moment it started growing exponentially was the global financial and economic crisis since 2008 (Hanemann and Huotari 2017). Since 2008, Chinese investments in the EU have grown by the factor of ten. In 2016 alone, Chinese FDI in the EU grew on the previous year by 77%. At the same time, EU FDI in China, which until 2013 was higher than Chinese FDI in the EU, in 2016, for the first time since 2000, significantly declined.

Roughly, EU recipient countries of Chinese FDI can be subdivided into three groups: The large economies in the West, with Germany and France in the middle; the more troubled economies of the southern tier, especially Portugal, Spain, Italy and Greece; and the often weak but recently more dynamic economies of the formerly communist 'new member states' on the eastern and southeastern flanks of the EU (partly overlapping with the '16 + 1' group of formerly communist countries inside and outside the EU). While in the years before 2008, the EU's core economies in Western Europe had been the main target, with the onset of the crisis, the Central and Eastern European countries, as well as the more peripheral West European economies, such as Greece, had moved into focus. But in 2016, the UK, France and Germany as well as the Nordic economies were back in their central position. This may be due to several factors, but above all, the focus on cash-strapped eastern or southern EU member states may have receded in favour of the bigger and more dynamic economies because of the increasing Chinese emphasis on 'buying technology' (especially in Germany). Hence, within just one year, from 2015 to 2016, Chinese FDI in Germany increased almost ten-fold to 11 billion euros, going predominantly to innovative and high-tech sectors. For the 16 + 1 countries, the gigantic 'Belt and Road Initiative' infrastructure project is a major driver for Chinese FDI into road, rail and other 'connectivity'.

Europe's Key Interests

Whether at all, and if yes, in what sense, the rapid increase in China's FDI in Europe is seen as a problem depends strongly on the EU member state in question: For instance, public opinion in most EU countries except Great Britain is, in varying degrees, suspicious of foreign investments in general and foreign acquisitions of local firms in particular, hence also of Chinese FDI.

The EU's interests as to Chinese FDI largely consist of three points, in descending order of priority:

- *Preserving liberal democracy* and avoiding political dependence on others: Irrespective of how threatened liberal democracy and the rule of law may be inside the EU in cases such as Hungary and Poland, there is every reason to defend the values upon which the EU is built, from all outside attempts to weaken them as well.
- *Maximising economic profit*—this is closely related to reciprocity: A legitimate goal of all economic activity, profit maximisation here means looking at the gain not only from selling assets to a buyer, but also from being able to acquire them in the buyer's own country. That is what is so ominous about the increasingly difficult conditions

for foreign investors in China itself, while Chinese investments abroad are booming. Also, keeping a competitive edge through preserving technological superiority is an important factor of profit maximisation, especially in a situation in which labour costs outside the EU are mostly so much lower.

- *Safeguarding European standards* in environment, labour, and so on: While foreign investors, as a matter of course, have to follow existing laws and regulations in Europe, there are fears that their investments, in combination with political pressure and increasing control over key sectors of the economy, could lead to a watering down of standards. This may well be the remotest of concerns for the moment, but at least in public opinion, not the least relevant.

More specifically, the concrete concerns connected to Chinese FDI (Hellström 2016) fall into five categories:

- *Political influence—weakening coherence*: First and foremost, there are fears that Chinese influence through growing investments lead to division lines between and inside member states, especially when policies vis-à-vis China are concerned. China is quite evidently trying to wield political influence through many instruments, not least through FDI. One of the most blatant examples is the Greek veto in the EU Council against an EU resolution critical of Chinese territorial expansionism in the South China Sea in the summer of 2016, after the Chinese investor COSCO assumed control of the port of Piraeus near Athens. EU resolutions critical of China's human rights record regularly meet with resistance from Greece and Hungary, both of whom have been very much recipients of Chinese FDI. What is remarkable is that in these cases of direct political influence through FDI, it is practically irrelevant whether the investments have been made by a 'private' or a state-owned Chinese company (Duesterberg 2018a). In any case, it may safely be assumed that no acquisition of major foreign assets happens without the knowledge and approval of the CCP.
- *Control of assets with relevance to national security*: This concerns particularly so-called dual-use technologies in advanced fields, such as artificial intelligence, robotics and so forth, as well as critical infrastructure and media. China's bid to acquire Germany's computer chip equipment maker Aixtron through the Chinese company Fujian was blocked by the Berlin Economic Ministry in October 2016

(Duesterberg 2018b). In the case of German robot maker KUKA, the sale to the Chinese household manufacturer Midea eventually took place despite attempts by the German government to limit the transfer of shares to 49%. The concerns here are that Chinese acquisitions are used to gain key technologies, which are transferred to China and then used to gain further competitive advantages against Western firms. In France, there has been a lively debate in recent years regarding sales of nuclear power stations and critical airport infrastructure to Chinese investors. Media are a special case; here, it's not technology that is in the focus of concerns but political influence: Chinese acquisitions in Czech media in recent years have, in combination with direct political influence via President Milos Zeman and his entourage (including Chinese advisors), arguably led to a much more favourable reporting on China in Czech mainstream media (Benner et al. 2018).

- Chinese corporate governance and business practices: This refers mainly to increased delocalisation of jobs, but also to accusations of fraud, wage suppression and undermining of collective bargaining of trade unions.
- Lack of reciprocity in market openness: Precisely in many of the sectors in Europe preferred by Chinese FDI, in China itself, state-owned and state-supported enterprises are given precedence by government authorities when wanting to acquire assets. That is true not only for all matters high-tech, but also for financial services.
- CCP links: As stated above, the CCP is the ultimate arbiter in all crucial parts of Chinese business. That includes, of course, Chinese overseas FDI. The recent increasingly openly operating CCP cells in European investments in China itself have further highlighted this problem.

The Instruments of the EU and Its Member States

Less than half of the (currently) 28 member states of the EU have any national screening processes for foreign investment: Austria, Denmark, Germany, Finland, France, Latvia, Lithuania, Italy, Poland, Portugal, Spain and the UK. But even among those, there is no consensus about any executive power for the EU to intervene in foreign acquisitions, for various political and economic reasons. The UK and other northwestern EU members come from an economic philosophy which emphasises free and open markets, and they are traditionally averse to any state intervention in the economy, of course including FDI. In the south, it is the general need for investment, often to make up for lack of financial inflows from Europe itself, which makes governments close their eyes to the challenges posed by Chinese FDI—national investment screening notwithstanding. Intervention from Brussels is not welcome in these cases, to say the least. The same is true for formerly communist countries in Central Europe, where real or perceived interference from Brussels has, rightly or wrongly, acquired a particularly ominous connotation. Hungary and Poland are remarkable cases in this sense: In FIDESZ-led Hungary under Viktor Orban since 2010, Chinese credits and FDI have deliberately been used to offset an 'overbearing' EU and the International Monetary Fund (IMF), which, in the view of the Hungarian government, cared too much about the rule of law and other principles distrusted by Hungary's leadership. Moreover, at least since his notorious speech extolling the virtues of the 'illiberal state' in the summer of 2014, suspicions have been raised about a certain degree of admiration by Orban for some aspects of the Chinese model of economic and social development. Poland under 'Law and Justice' (PiS), on the other hand, has been tempted to use Chinese investments in order to 'escape' from the strategic challenges of depending on 'Brussels' and the alleged geostrategic 'squeeze' between Germany and Russia, which exists at least in the imagination of the strongman behind the Polish government, Jaroslaw Kaczynski.

Consequently, any attempt to rise to the Chinese FDI challenge on the EU level must tread carefully. The response must begin with EU institutions and fellow member states encouraging their partners to introduce—and actually implement and apply—national guidelines for FDI screening.

As the debate about Chinese FDI intensified, more and more EU politicians, officials and experts woke up to the need for an EU-wide screening mechanism. The decisive development in this respect happened during 2017: In April of that year, the economic ministers of Italy, France and Germany wrote a joint letter to Commissioner Malmström, arguing for an EU framework, for the European Commission proposal represents a compromise between the different strategic approaches in the EU. Since then, the Commission has been working on a mechanism to increase information sharing and cooperation when faced with strategic FDI.

In particular, the approach focuses on

- more transparency between member states and the Commission;
- a higher awareness of the security implications of FDI in strategic sectors of the economy, especially in countries without national screening mechanisms; and
- introducing direct screening of FDI in projects involving EU funding or established through EU legislation.

The Council will decide about the Commission's proposal before the end of 2018. Predictably, the main challenges among the member states come from 'free marketeers' and cash-strapped southern and eastern member states. Consequently, even the already cautious approach by the European Commission may be further watered down (Godement and Vasselier 2017).

Such a mechanism would at least address one major weakness among EU member states when faced with Chinese strategic investment: the near-total lack of indigenous China expertise, independent of Chinese financing, among precisely those countries in the east and south which—for different reasons—feel the strongest need for capital inflows. This gap could at least partly be remedied by the solid information exchange that would be part of an EU-wide screening mechanism (Rasmussen Global n.d.).

Furthermore, since 2015, the European Commission has been working on an investment agreement with China which addresses the lack of an even playing field in mutual FDI. Such a Bilateral Investment Treaty (BIT), coming on top of several existing bilateral ones between EU member states and China, would guarantee better access of European investors to precisely those sectors of the Chinese market that are most closed, such as high-tech and financial services. However, given China's increasing penchant for unilateralism in relations to the EU, the chances of such an agreement to seriously level the playing field are limited.

Conclusions

Foreign direct investment per se is a good thing and a decisive ingredient of the economic and cultural exchange that has become an elementary part of human progress. But China's strategic FDI in Europe since 2008, and in the future, has to be seen as part of its larger foreign strategy, aiming not only at economic gain and technological advantage but also at political control of other countries.

It must be addressed without bias against the Chinese nation or culture. But it should be addressed with firmness, at EU level as well as on the level of individual member states. A European response to the Chinese FDI challenge must be embedded in a larger EU response to the strategic challenge by China, which is best characterised by the term 'sharp power'.

This begins with a much more decisive effort at developing and promoting China expertise independent of Chinese funding. National governments as well as EU institutions, especially the European Commission, have a decisive role to play in providing funds and encouragement.

The core of the EU's response should be a screening mechanism for FDI, designed to enhance existing national mechanisms and encourage their creation where they do not yet exist. This would facilitate the exchange of information and lead to common definitions of potential threats to security and the fundamental interests of the EU and its member states in view of FDI. Optimally, this will make it harder for China to exercise its 'sharp power' by means of strategic investments while preserving the economic advantages of FDI.

Finally, in the effort to respond to the FDI challenge, the EU and its member states need to operate as part of the Western alliance and work with like-minded partners, both in the West and among China's immediate neighbours. This may look difficult in the era of President Trump, but it must nevertheless be tried.

References

Benner, Thorsten, Jan Gaspers, Mareike Ohlberg, Lucrezia Poggetti, and Kristin Shi-Kupfer, Authoritarian Advance—Responding to China's Growing Political Influence in Europe, Berlin 2018. Accessed June 24, 2018. http://www.gppi.net/publications/rising-powers/article/authoritarian-advance-responding-to-chinas-growing-political-influence-in-europe/

Duesterberg, Thomas J., 5G: China's Dream to Dominate World Technology, Hudson Institute, Washington, DC, 2018a. Accessed June 24, 2018. https://www.hudson.org/research/14071-5-g-china-s-dream-to-dominate-world-technology

Duesterberg, Thomas J., Chinese Economic and Trade Challenges to the West: Prospects and Consequences from a U.S.-German Perspective, Hudson Institute/Konrad Adenauer Stiftung, Washington, DC, 2018b. Accessed June 24, 2018. https://www.hudson.org/research/14150-chinese-economic-and-trade-challenges-to-the-west-prospects-and-consequences-from-a-u-s-german-perspective

Godement, Francois, and Abigail Vasselier, China at the gates: A new power audit of EU-China relations, ECFR, London, December 2017. Accessed June 24, 2018. http://www.ecfr.eu/publications/summary/china_eu_power_audit7242

Hanemann, Thilo, and Mikko Huotari, Record Flows and Growing Imbalances—Chinese Investment in Europe in 2016, MERICS Papers on China Update No. 3, Berlin 2017. Accessed June 24, 2018. http://rhg.com/wp-content/uploads/2017/01/RHG_Merics_COFDI_EU_2016.pdf

Hellström, Jerker, China's Acquisitions in Europe—European Perceptions of Chinese Investments and their Strategic Implications, FOI Stockholm, 2016. Accessed June 24, 2018. https://www.researchgate.net/publication/315497771_China's_Acquisitions_in_Europe_European_Perceptions_of_Chinese_Investments_and_their_Strategic_Implications

Rasmussen Global, Foreign Investment Screening and the China Factor—New protectionism or new European standards? (n.d.). Accessed June 24, 2018. https://rasmussenglobal.com/media/foreign-investment-screening-china-factor-memo

CHAPTER 10

China: A Partner for Today and for the Future?

Thorsten Frei

China's Rise to Economic Superpower

In the 40 years since the end of the Cultural Revolution, China has accomplished astonishingly rapid economic development, which is reflected in all areas of society. After Deng Xiaoping's first attempts to open up the country in 1978, China has undergone several waves of modernisation and industrialisation in a process which took several centuries in Europe. China's gross domestic product (GDP) has more than tripled in this space of time. More than 700 million people have been lifted out of poverty. In 2017 alone there were ten million fewer Chinese living below the poverty line of a per capita GDP of 500 US dollars. The country has had impressive success in its efforts to tackle poverty. It is now the world's largest economy, and by 2014, it had already overtaken the USA in terms of GDP adjusted for relative purchasing power.

The "Made in China 2020" strategy and the associated extensive concentration on research and development are an indication that the country is on course for further growth and prosperity. More than 2500 basic

T. Frei (✉)
German Bundestag, Berlin, Germany
e-mail: thorsten.frei@bundestag.de

T. Wenniges, W. Lohman (eds.), *Chinese FDI in the EU and the US*,
https://doi.org/10.1007/978-981-13-6071-8_10

patents were taken out between 2013 and 2015, supporting data from the American National Science Foundation, which put China in the number two spot for investment in knowledge and innovation. Between 2010 and 2018 investment in research rose by around 18% per year. Chinese contributions to technical journals are also growing steadily in terms of both quality and quantity. It is expected that, in this area too, China will lead the field in ten years' time.

The state, of course, exercises an entirely different influence in China than is the case in Germany and the other Western democracies. Nevertheless China's achievements are undeniable. To attribute this success solely to imitation and the theft of intellectual property is too easy. China could not have achieved the greatest reduction in poverty in human history without observing market economy rules, without instituting reforms, without creating greater legal certainty, without clearly opening up the country and without the hard work of its people. Such a reading would likewise ignore the history of other industrialised nations which also developed through a process of imitation and improvement.

A study carried out by analysts from PricewaterhouseCoopers into changes in the economic order clearly illustrated that these developments have further to run. While China and the USA are virtually level today in terms of GDP, the picture up to 2050 shifts considerably. The USA, meanwhile overtaken by India, ranks only third among the largest economies. According to these projections it will achieve only about two thirds of China's economic power. Germany falls from fifth to tenth place and is the only remaining European country in the top ten.

The German Economy Needs China

Given such forecasts and the fact that China continues to contribute around 25% to global economic growth, it is clear that Germany, as the world's leading exporter at this time, benefits from China's high demand and has an interest in good economic relations.

Just how good these relations are can be seen from developments in foreign trade. Fifty-three years ago in 1965 Germany exported goods to the value of 162 million euros and imported goods to the value of 149 euros. Today the values for exports and imports stand at 86 and 100 billion euros, respectively, roughly 600 times higher than at that time.

As a market of almost 1.4 billion people, China is highly attractive for our economy. There is good reason why some 5000 German companies are doing business in China, 800 of them from my home state of Baden-Württemberg.

Given these developments it comes as no surprise that last year, as in 2016, the People's Republic was Germany's most important trading partner. Neither is it surprising that the business community has called for economic relations to be intensified in the face of the protectionist stance projected by the American president.

It is, nevertheless, important for us to recognise that in our globalised world, competition as a whole is growing tougher. It is vital for all companies equally to master the transition to a knowledge economy based on comprehensive digitalisation and networking. It would be fatal for our economy to rely on or focus too much on individual countries. This applies in particular to China, which, in a position of new strength, serves only its own interests and shows little willingness to engage in constructive multilateral cooperation.

The Dark Clouds Are Massing for German Companies

Apart from the omnipresent restrictions China imposes on its own population, the increasingly obvious strength of China's political leadership is most visible at present in the area of the economy. China is pursuing a proactive industrial policy deriving from a system of state subsidies for Chinese firms, the obligation to share technology as a prerequisite for market access and growing political controls on non-Chinese market participants.

No German company would be able to acquire a stake in a Chinese company without major problems or the consent of the political elites. More and more foreign companies are being forced into joint ventures even in areas which do not require this at all. The political leadership in Beijing is trying increasingly frequently to become actively involved in joint ventures and block corporate decisions it finds undesirable. Under pressure from political leaders joint venture contracts are adjusted to this effect. This has led in some cases to interference for party-political reasons in corporate decisions such as restructuring or redundancies dictated by commercial reasons. German companies have already had experience of this.

Even global players such as Apple, Google and Microsoft are now required to store their customer data internally in China and, as a result, to give the state unfettered access to this data as well as to provide access to source and security codes. Those who refuse can literally pack their bags and quit the Chinese market. This goes so far that cyber security laws are used to block access to the internet for foreign companies.

It is therefore not surprising that the past euphoria of German companies has drastically diminished and, conversely, the number of German companies asking for help from the German Embassy in Beijing has tripled over the past three years. In the last survey conducted by the German Chamber of Commerce Abroad, almost 40% of companies questioned stated they no longer felt as welcome as they did a few years ago. More than half did not plan any new investments in China and 12% were even thinking of quitting the country. These examples highlight the great difficulty in dealing with China. What on a small scale is a considerable annoyance for many companies is for us, as a cosmopolitan country geared to free trade, intolerable in the long term.

Neither is there anything to indicate that China will change course and institute the reforms which were still being promoted in 2013. The remaining vague hope probably evaporated at the latest Party Congress when, in addition to removing the time limit on Xi Jiping's term of office, various amendments to the constitution effectively buried the legacy of the reformer, Deng Xiaoping. Deng was convinced that China's economic forces could only be unleashed by separating the government and party. Now, however, the party once again exercises full control over the state and also claims the right to monitor and control everything in the economy as well.

The Openness of the West Is Being Mercilessly Exploited

As if this were not enough, Beijing is increasingly seeking to act outside its own borders to its own advantage. As in the past it is intent on strengthening its own economy by acquiring foreign hi-tech and intellectual property in legal ways, for example, through university cooperation agreements or by taking stakes in companies, but also demonstrably by way of cyber attacks. Everything is subordinated to the "Made in China 2025" strategy announced by the political leadership three year ago, which is aimed at giving China technological supremacy in the areas of robotics, artificial intelligence, semi-conductor technology and electrical drive systems.

Beijing's buying sprees in the past two years in particular have provoked broad debate in Germany. In 2017 China invested a fat 13.7 billion euros in German companies in 54 major transactions. These include the takeover of the energy provider ISTA by Cheung Kong Property, the stake taken by the HNA Group in Deutsche Bank and the acquisition of the pharmaceutical company Biotest. Particular controversy has surrounded the 10% stake taken by Geely in Daimler, circumventing legal reporting obligations, and also the takeover of KUKA last year, because they, more than any other transactions, show what interests China is pursuing and what means it is prepared to use. This applies particularly to the attempt by China to position its own satraps overseas, who can then sit on supervisory boards, influencing the strategic development of major companies—where possible in line with Beijing's interests—and gaining deep insights into business processes and technical secrets.

China Is Seeking System Conflict

It is becoming increasingly apparent, however, that the economy is only one area in which the Chinese leadership is operating to satisfy Beijing's growing hunger for power. China's striving for political power, too, is becoming ever more apparent not just in Southeast Asia—witness the Senkaku Islands dispute—but also in Europe.

It is true that political harassment from Moscow is omnipresent, not least because of its greater geographical proximity and Russia's overtly confrontational behaviour, as we have seen in the nerve agent attack in Great Britain, hacking attacks on the German government network and the destabilisation of Ukraine. In the medium-to-long term, however, the challenges posed by China—which, because of the way the state is organised, resolutely and openly rejects our values, our freedom and our democracy—are far greater as a result of its inordinately greater economic power and future economic dominance.

This is clear in the first place from the enticing initiative for a New Silk Road which promises to benefit all neighbouring countries, first and foremost by way of progress with infrastructure projects and economic participation. But this promise is nothing other than a Trojan horse. While it will undoubtedly facilitate infrastructure projects which many smaller countries would not otherwise be able to realise, this will happen almost exclusively to China's advantage. China is extending loans to finance projects. Chinese construction companies are awarded most of the contracts, and even the majority of construction workers employed come from China. It can be safely said, therefore, that the New Silk Road initiative is one thing above all else: a stimulus programme for China's economy in increasingly uncertain times when China is having more and more difficulty in matching the growth figures of recent times and hence fulfilling the plans of the Communist Party.

Furthermore, investments which are often negotiated under the spotlight of diplomacy between the leaders of the countries involved are designed to enable China actively to help shape policy in Europe or to block undesirable decisions, for example, in the areas of commerce or human rights issues. This is relatively straightforward because of the way the EU functions and the associated veto rights of individual member states.

It may be a coincidence, but shortly after the Port of Piraeus was taken over by a Chinese investor, the Greek government blocked a joint EU resolution with respect to China in the United Nations (UN) Human Rights Council. There are countless other examples of China attempting to gain the goodwill of the political class through generous investments. This applies to the EU 27 as well as to the countries of the Western Balkans, which are looking to join the EU and which, if the EU Treaties are not amended, could, despite having the smallest populations, be responsible for crucial blocking actions.

China is also seeking to place influencers in many key positions in politics, business, science and the media and in civil society who consciously or unconsciously represent Beijing's interests. This has gone so far that China has directly installed an advisor in the office of President Milos Zeman in the Czech Republic.

There are three key factors here. Firstly the Chinese leadership wants to gain power and influence in order to shape developments to its own advantage and, in so doing, open up access to markets, knowledge and raw materials. Ultimately there is nothing it hates more than unpredictable surprises, opposing opinions and decisions which are not controlled centrally by the party.

This is why, secondly, it is a central goal of China to weaken the unity between the liberal democracies of the West, both within Europe and in the transatlantic alliance. Ultimately China, along with Russia and Iran, rejects our democracy and our way of life. The problem is that countries such as these believe our democracy represents a threat to their own autocratic systems. The freedom of people here reinforces the lack of social legitimation there. That is why they seek, in many different ways, to delegitimise and destabilise our country and the West.

Thirdly and consequently, Beijing strives wherever possible to convey a positive picture of centrally controlled state capitalism as a successful political and economic model, and present it as a respectable alternative to the democracy which is being increasingly questioned in the West. Its aim is to ensure the legitimacy of the Communist Party at home.

What is noticeable in this process is that China is presenting an increasingly self-confident image and challenging and casting doubt on the Western liberal order more and more openly. In doing so, it is cleverly and systematically exploiting the openness of our economic and political system to its own advantage while strenuously ejecting foreign ideas and players or foreign capital and opinions from its own sphere.

The West Must Respond with One Voice and with Resolve

We increasingly find ourselves, therefore, in a competition between systems. It is crystal clear to me that Europe must not under any circumstances resort to retaliation and copy China's protectionist approach—as US President Donald Trump is attempting to do.

Ultimately our continent benefits from openness, diversity, competition and freedom. They are the DNA which make Europe and Germany strong. This is why I recommend that we maintain the greatest possible openness going forward into the future. We must also, in the face of increasingly difficult circumstances, continue to believe in and openly champion our liberal values. These values ultimately have a magnetic power which, despite censorship and restriction, radiates as far as East Asia.

At the same time, however, we must not be naive or blind. We must not allow ourselves to be left out or politically blocked. To pursue a forward-looking and responsible policy it is essential that we look beyond short-term sales advantages and do not generously turn a blind eye to undesirable developments and challenges created by the Chinese side. This would be a fatal mistake if we are to preserve Europe's prosperity.

Rather we must accept these challenges and develop strategies to halt China's rapidly growing influence within the EU.

First and foremost the federal government must continue openly and resolutely to insist to the Chinese that fair competition conditions and reciprocity are the key to an economic win-win situation. We must not and will not accept state-imposed dumping prices or restrictions to market access, since these damage our economy and businesses. As an open economy, we place our reliance on free and fair exchange.

In relation to world trade, America and Europe need to close ranks to rein in China and maintain the liberal order of the World Trade Organization (WTO). China itself has been a member of the WTO since 2001 and is therefore obliged to abide strictly by the established rules. But since it adopts a deeply protectionist stance in its home market and floods other markets with subsidised goods, it has progressively undermined and upset the proven body of rules under which the WTO operates. As a consequence trust in the WTO has been increasingly eroded. Unfortunately there is no sign at the present time of any such coming together in the transatlantic relationship.

But we can also do something nationally, since simply talking will not help us in the end. In certain cases we need specific bans and restrictions in order to make us less susceptible to influence.

As a first step by the federal government, in reaction to the takeover of KUKA, manufacturer of industrial robots and factory automation systems, by the Chinese company Midea, the Foreign Trade and Payments Regulation has been amended, extending the right of veto applying to company takeovers by third countries and protecting key German technologies. For the first time this provides a concrete measure to remedy a possible risk to public order through company takeovers where these concern critical infrastructure, as in the case of hospitals or the water or power supply. Although in the roughly 40 test cases examined by the Federal Ministry for Economic Affairs to date, there have been no rejections, operators are better protected against the involvement of investors from outside the EU and the government has more time to veto a possible sale.

But other investments and takeovers too, such as the stake taken by the Chinese investor Geely in Daimler, show that, where possible, we need to tighten regulations. That is why it is right that Peter Altmaier, Federal Minister of Economic Affairs, is currently examining whether, in future, Germany can intervene in cases in which foreign investors take over only 10% rather than the current 25% of shares in a German company.

There must be better protection in future for key technologies. A ban on sales is already being far more rigorously implemented in the USA than here in Germany. Certain foreign companies and investors are openly designated as a security risk there. Just recently AT&T was forced to end a cooperation agreement with Huawei. Products from certain Chinese telecommunications companies, including ZTE, may no longer be used in government offices in the US administration. Here Germany must also act more resolutely. The same applies to the fight against political and economic cyber espionage.

Besides protecting businesses and the economy, however, we can also do more as a society and strengthen resilience against Chinese influence. For this to succeed, awareness of China, Chinese policy and also culture needs to be raised in Europe. The first important element for this is to boost research into contemporary China. Creating broad awareness in dealing with Chinese players—whether at official state level with respect to the smaller EU member states or at social and cultural level in Germany—can only be achieved on the basis of facts and an objective analysis of Beijing's policy. Where Europe is concerned, we must attach greater importance to the value of the community. This also means that, if necessary, we must invest more and we must continue to make it clear that what motivates us is the wish to ensure a good future for Europe and a good future for every European. China does not offer this.

It is not very helpful in this context to see the bosses of tech giants going on pilgrimage to internet conferences in China despite the fact that the Great Firewall of China blocks or even bans the use of their products such as Skype or email programs. By doing this they thwart efforts to unmask Chinese censorship and, for pure monetary gain, throw our Western values overboard.

It is also worth considering imposing stricter obligations of disclosure with respect to Chinese involvement in and funding of events or the work of non-governmental organisations and also tightening rules on party funding through a general ban on donations from outside Germany.

Involving Countries of the Region

In terms of a holistic strategy for China we must also look to the East. China certainly has very many business partners as a result of the Silk Road Initiative and the associated investment promises. Since, however, it is implementing these projects in a very heavy-handed way, in line with the overriding objectives of the "China First" policy, and thus has no real friends or allies. The majority of neighbours and countries in the region are very concerned about China's ambitions and its current armament programme. There is scope here to develop a counterweight through negotiations and economic cooperation with India and Japan, in particular.

This has nothing to do, however, with provoking conflict. In our multipolar world what we need instead are careful balances. Despite all the assurances of the basic peaceful direction of its foreign policy, China is creating a dangerous imbalance. At this juncture there is a need to hold the leadership under Xi Jinping to its own statements and persuade China, as a veto power in the UN Security Council, to become more involved in the resolution of intractable problems such as the civil war in Syria, the conflict in Afghanistan or the nuclear disputes with Iran and North Korea. From the European perspective this is unfortunately difficult to imagine at the present time and then, as outlined, only within very narrow limits.

CHAPTER 11

China's Outbound Investments and the Rule of Law

Lutz-Christian Wolff

Introduction

Since the end of the last century China's outbound investments have developed at a breathtaking pace.[1] China is often criticized for its aggressive investment strategies for a variety of reasons, last but not least for not adhering to the rule of law. This chapter explores the relationship between China's outbound investment activities and the rule of law. It is divided into five sections. Following these introductory remarks some basic background information is provided on the past development and current status of China's outbound investments. The third section then introduces the rule of law doctrine from a general point of view, followed by a discus-

[1] For details compare *infra*, Sect. 2.

Wei Lun Professor of Law & Dean of Graduate School, The Chinese University of Hong Kong, email: wolff@cuhk.edu.hk. Online sources quoted in the following were last visited on 11 April 2018. Thanks for good research support go to Jenny Chan.

L.-C. Wolff (✉)
The Chinese University of Hong Kong, Hong Kong, China
e-mail: wolff@cuhk.edu.hk

T. Wenniges, W. Lohman (eds.), *Chinese FDI in the EU and the US*,
https://doi.org/10.1007/978-981-13-6071-8_11

sion of the status of the rule of law in China. The main section of this chapter discusses the significance of the rule of law for the success of Chinese outbound investment projects. Some final remarks of a more general nature conclude this chapter.

Chinese Outbound Investments

As Chinese outbound investments are the main theme of this book there is no need for this chapter to present related data in a comprehensive way. However, to set the scene for the subsequent discussion of related rule of law implications, some key aspects shall be highlighted in the following.[2]

While the Chinese central government had adopted a "going-out policy" during the second half of the 1990s with the goal to encourage Chinese enterprises to invest abroad, during the ten-year period from 1990 to 2000, the annual volume of Chinese investments overseas was on average only around US$3 billion.[3] The picture changed dramatically after the beginning of the new millennium, but developments were slowed down again as a result of the global financial crisis.[4] Substantial government support in the form of a stimulus package of RMB4 trillion[5] helped China's economy to recover quickly. It also re-invigorated China's outbound investment activities. Taking advantage of the fact that the global financial crisis had left many overseas companies in urgent need of capital injections, China's outbound investment volume increased significantly. And China's outbound activities were arguably also a major factor that helped other economies to overcome the problems caused by the global financial crisis.

In 2016 China's outbound investment volume was globally the second largest, tailing only the US.[6] In the same year Chinese investments had targeted 6236 foreign enterprises in 174 countries.[7] Between 2014 and

[2] Compare for the following Lutz-Christian Wolff, Mergers & Acquisitions in China: Law and Practice, 5th ed. (Hong Kong: Wolters Kluwer, 2015), pp. 217–230.

[3] Ibid., p. 217.

[4] Ibid.

[5] Ibid., *supra* note 2, p. 218; also compare Lutz-Christian Wolff, Chinese Investments Overseas—Onshore Rules and Offshore Risks, The International Lawyer, Vol. 45 (No. 4) (Winter 2011), pp. 1029–1049 (1031); Lutz-Christian Wolff (ed.), China Outbound Investments—A Guide to Law and Practice (Hong Kong: CCH Hong Kong Limited, 2011), p. 1.

[6] UNCTAD, World Investment Report 2017, p. 14, at http://unctad.org/en/PublicationChapters/wir2017ch1_en.pdf.

[7] PRC Ministry of Commerce, at http://english.mofcom.gov.cn/article/statistic/foreigntradecooperation/201802/20180202715839.shtml.

2016 China had taken steps to facilitate outbound investment activities by liberalizing the governing legal regime.[8] It is noteworthy, however, that in light of apparently uncontrolled outflows of large sums of money to foreign destinations and concerns regarding the viability of many outbound investment projects starting from 2015, government authorities re-introduced and tightened control mechanisms.[9] In 2017 China's total outbound investment volume therefore saw a decline by 29.4% year on year to US$120.08 billion as a result of

> draconian curbs on outbound investment and capital outflows since the stock market rout in the summer of 2015.[10]

Chinese outbound investments have received considerable attention in recent times. This is not only a result of national security concerns raised in actual and potential target countries, but also because of fears that Chinese investments in high-tech industries will allow Chinese companies to outplay their Western competitors in due course.[11] Furthermore, China's "Belt and Road initiative", which was announced in 2013 and

[8] See Wolff (2015), *supra* note 2, pp. 217–230; Latham & Watkins, China Issues Formal Guidance for Outbound Direct Investments (30 August 2017), at https://www.lw.com/thoughtLeadership/LW-China-Issues-Formal-Guidance-for-Outbound-Direct-Investments.

[9] Compare Stephen D. Wortley et al., China's Capital Controls—Implications for China Focused Companies (January 2017), http://mcmillan.ca/Chinas-Capital-Controls-Implications-for-China-Focused-Companies, p. 1; Angus Grigg/Lisa Murray, China tightens controls on moving money overseas, Financial Review 20 January 2016, at http://www.afr.com/news/world/asia/china-tightens-controls-on-moving-money-overseas-20160120-gma7g3; Latham & Watkins, ibid.; Clifford Chance, PRC State Council Issues Guidelines on Overseas Investments (September 2017), at https://financialmarketstoolkit.cliffordchance.com/en/financial-markets-resources/resources-by-type/client-briefings/2017/09/prc-state-council-issues-guidelines-on-overseas-investments%2D%2Dsep.html; Clifford Chance, China Introduces New Rules on Outbound Investment (January 2018), at https://www.cliffordchance.com/briefings/2018/01/china_introducesnewrulesonoutboundinvestment.html.

[10] Eugene Tang/Zhou Xin, World Requires Debt Correction, IMF Head Warns, SCMP 12 April 2018, p. A1.

[11] Georg Blume, Trumps Sorgen wegen China sind berechtigt (Trump's concerns regarding China are justified), Spiegel online 13 April 2018, at http://www.spiegel.de/wirtschaft/soziales/donald-trump-im-handelskrieg-seine-sorgen-wegen-china-sind-berechtigt-a-1202091.html, citing growing concerns of the West to be in an economically inferior position toward China in the future; Wang Xiangwei, Trump's trade war is just a gambit—here's what's next, SCMP—This Week in Asia 15–21 April 2018, pp. 10–11 (10).

aims to connect China and countries along the ancient Silk Road, will increase Chinese investments in particular in infrastructure projects in Central and South Asia significantly.[12] While many features of the Belt and Road initiative are still uncertain,[13] it has become apparent that its impact could be significant. The Belt and Road initiative covers 50% of the world's population, 40% of the world's gross domestic product and 75% of the known energy resources.[14]

There has been a lot of speculation about the motives behind China's outbound activities, including the Belt and Road initiative. It is on the one hand not surprising that overseas investment projects of Chinese multinational enterprises are driven by self-interest, including economic, geopolitical, military[15] and strategic goals. In fact, access to uninterrupted food

[12] Compare Lutz-Christian Wolff, China's "Belt and Road" Initiative—An Introduction, in Lutz-Christian Wolff/Chao Xi, Legal Dimensions of China's Belt and Road Initiative (Hong Kong: Wolters Kluwer, 2016), pp. 1–31. According to the People's Republic of China Ministry of Commerce, the volume of Chinese non-financial direct investments in Belt and Road countries went up by 50% year on year in January 2018 to US$1.23 billion. The main target countries were Singapore, Malaysia, Laos, Vietnam, Indonesia, Pakistan, Sri Lanka and Iran; see http://english.mofcom.gov.cn/article/statistic/foreigntradecooperation/201802/20180202715869.shtml; compare for problems of Belt and Road countries to finance-involved infrastructure projects, Hu Huifeng, Silk Road projects hit financing roadblocks, SCMP 15 April 2018, p. A5.

[13] Lutz-Christian Wolff, From a 'Small Phrase with Big Ambitions' to a Powerful Driver of Contract Law Unification?—China's Belt and Road Initiative and the CISG, 34 (Part 1) Journal of Contract Law (2017), pp. 50–69, 51–54; Bob Savic, Belt and road is a political, as well as economic, force, SCMP 27 November 2017, p. A11: "The belt and road scheme will play a role policymakers may not have envisaged, but it is part of a greater, multidimensional set of relations. These are guided by Beijing's constantly evolving bilateral strategic partnerships, which may prove essential in enabling China to deal with challenges along the many diverse, historically volatile countries along the belt and road network".

[14] Julia Hollingsworth, Trade Body Sees a Bigger Belt and Road, SCMP 19 September 2016, p. B6; compare Central Committee of the Communist Party of China (CPC), Recommendations for the 13th Five-Year Plan for Economic and Social Development (Central Compilation & Translation Press, Beijing December 2015) 20; PRC National Development and Reform Commission/PRC Ministry of Foreign Affairs/PRC Ministry of Commerce (with State Council authorization), Vision and Actions on Jointly Building Silk Road Economic Belt and 21st-Century Maritime Silk Road, News Release, 28 March 2015, English version available at NDRC, http://en.ndrc.gov.cn/newsrelease/201503/t20150330_669367.html, under VI. China's Regions in Pursing Opening Up.

[15] Compare Associated Press, Why the U.S. is alarmed by China's Africa deals, SCMP 11 March 2018, p. A10; Wolff (2011), in The International Lawyer, *supra* note 5, p. 1048.

supply,[16] energy, natural resources and rare earths is crucial for the development of China's economy and the Chinese society as such.[17] On the other hand, Chinese overseas investments must also be seen as a natural consequence of the development of the Chinese economy, which has reached a level at which globalization is the natural next step.[18]

The Rule of Law Doctrine

China has often been criticized for not adhering to the rule of law. This section therefore first briefly recaps core features of the rule of law doctrine.[19] It then discusses the status of the rule of law in China.

The rule of law doctrine stands at the core of many Western legal systems. Terminology[20] and doctrinal specifics differ, however, and have led to sometimes fierce debates among scholars and practitioners even within the same jurisdiction. The most fundamental disagreement concerns the question if the rule of law is to be understood in a purely formal way or if it also concerns fundamental substantive rights. Those who understand the rule of law in a purely formal way, that is, who adopt a narrow and thus so-called thin rule of law approach, (only) demand that legal systems have to guarantee

> a set of minimal characteristics: law must be set forth in advance (be prospective), be made public, be general, be stable and certain and be applied to everyone according to its terms.[21]

[16] Lutz-Christian Wolff, Chinese Outbound Investments in the Food Sector: Hungry for Much More!, 69 Food and Drug Law Journal (No. 3—2014), pp. 399–428.

[17] Compare Benesch Friedlaender Coplan Aranoff, China Goes Global: Examining China's Outbound Investment, China Insights January 2010, http://www.beneschlaw.com/Files/Publication/58b1c8f1-d679-4051-b50f-4631d1cac3b4/Presentation/PublicationAttachment/309b0f83-98ba-4ee8-b03f-46526897d787/January_2010.pdf; from the viewpoint of the Belt and Road initiative, Kingling Lo, The Netherlands calls for belt and road openness, SCMP 12 April 2018, p. A4: "To date, no Western European countries have partnered with China on its initiative, intended to expand connectivity in Eurasia by building infrastructure and trade routes. Britain, France and Germany have expressed scepticism about China's political goals for the project".

[18] Wolff (2015), *supra* note 2, p. 220.

[19] Compare for the following Lutz-Christian Wolff, Flexible Choice-of-Law Rules: Panacea or Oxymoron?, Journal of Private International Law Vol. 10 Number 3 (December 2014), pp. 431–459 (436–442).

[20] For example, in Germany, the term "Rechtsstaatsprinzip" is used.

[21] Brian Tamanaha, A Concise Guide to the Rule of Law (September 2007), available at http://www.ruleoflawus.info/The%20Rule/Tamanha%20Concise%20Guide%20to%20Rule%20of%20Law.pdf, p. 4.

These formal features of the rule of law, which form the basis of any (thin or thick) rule of law definition,[22] are important because they ensure that law is predictable in relation to its application outcomes and thus ensure legal certainty. Legal certainty in turn guarantees that in like circumstances, persons are treated alike, that the legal consequences of any behavior are known by everybody[23] and that rules are thus applied in a non-arbitrary way.[24] Adherence to the rule of law of course also implies that rules and regulations are applied as they are set. And as far as the addressees of rules and regulations are concerned, respect for the rule of law implies that rules and regulations are observed.

Thin rule of law concepts are criticized because they do not say anything

> about how the law is to be made: by tyrants, democratic majorities, or any other way. ... (They also) say(s) nothing about fundamental rights, about equality, or justice.[25]

It is for this reason that those who promote "thicker" rule of law understandings argue that in addition to the purely formal aspects, the rule of law also requires a minimum standard of basic rights, democracy and/or specific aspects of justice.[26] Details are again highly disputed around the world.

In China[27] the rule of law doctrine was not well known, and the knowledge and skills to implement this concept in practice did not exist at the beginning of the reform process in 1978.[28] The situation has of course changed over the years and the rule of law has become a very hotly debated

[22] Ibid.

[23] Ibid., p. 8.

[24] Compare ibid., pp. 9–10; Charles R. Calleros, Toward Harmonization and Certainty in Choice-of-Law Rules for International Contracts: Should the U.S. Adopt the Equivalent to Rome I?, (2010–2011) 28 Wisconsin International Law Journal, pp. 639–704 (670).

[25] Joseph Raz, The Rule of Law and its Virtue, in Aileen Kavanagh/John Oberdiek (eds.), Arguing about Law (London/New York: Routledge, 2009), pp. 181–192 (183) (reprint from Joseph Raz, The Authority of Law (Oxford: Clarendon Press, 1979), pp. 210–229).

[26] Ibid.

[27] For the following see Lutz-Christian Wolff, The Flexibility of Chinese Law—Trick or Treat for the "Belt and Road" Initiative, in: Wolff/Xi, *supra* note 12, pp. 593–625 (600–612).

[28] Compare Chang Wejen, Foreword, in: Karen G. Turner/James V. Feinerman/R. Kent Guy (eds.), The Limits of the Rule of Law in China (Seattle/London: University of Washington Press, 2000), p. xii.

topic in recent years also in China.[29] In 2014 China's National People's Congress and the Chinese People's Political Consultative Conference expressly mentioned the importance of the rule of law, provoking more discussions and leading to "unprecedented global attention".[30]

Nevertheless, in China, the rule of law doctrine is still not commonly accepted. Chinese academics have often argued that the rule of law doctrine is a Western concept which may not be in line with China's needs last but not least because law plays a different rule in the Chinese society.[31] Some have even warned that the rule of law is potentially capitalist in nature[32] and may contradict the leadership claim of the Chinese Communist Party.[33] Many commentators have suggested that China rather needs a "rule of law doctrine with Chinese characteristics".[34]

In China the rule of law does in fact not play the role it plays in Western societies. One may argue that this is, among others, a result of a continuing lack of awareness of its benefits, legal knowledge and skills or the unwillingness to implement the rule of law. In other cases law may have been abused for the sake of serving the interests of particular people or groups of people. Corruption[35] and local protectionism[36] are examples in

[29] Randall Peerenboom, Let One Hundred Flowers Bloom, One Hundred Schools Contend: Debating Rule of Law in China, 23 Michigan Journal of International Law (2002), pp. 471–574.

[30] Chen Qun, A New Perspective on the Rule of Law in China, China & US Focus (24 March 2014), https://www.chinausfocus.com/political-social-development/a-new-perspective-on-the-rule-of-law-in-china.

[31] Compare 陈超 (CHEN Chao), 中西传统政治文化的比较与启示 (Comparison and Revelation of the Rule of the Traditional Political Culture in China and the West), 福建农林大学学报(哲学社会科学版) (Journal of Fujian Agriculture and Forestry University (Philosophy and Social Sciences)) (Vol. 11) No 6 (2008), pp. 109–113 (112); Randall P. Peerenboom, China's Long March Toward the Rule of Law (Cambridge: Cambridge University Press, 2002), pp. 126–187.

[32] 柏維春、王玉华 (BO Weichun &WANG Yuhua), 中西传统政治文化中法治观念之比较 (Comparison of the Rule of Law Viewpoints in Terms of Traditional Political Culture in China and the West), 长白学刊 (Changbai Xuekan) (Vol 4) 2000, pp. 28–31 (31).

[33] Compare Margaret Y.K. Woo, Law and Discretion in the Contemporary Chinese Courts, 8 Pacific Rim Law & Policy Journal (1999), pp. 581–615 (592).

[34] 社会转型与法治建设 (The society's changing nature and the establishment of the legal system), in 诸葛平 (ZHU Geping) (ed.), 中国法律年鉴 (Chinese Yearbook of Law) 2011, p. 760.

[35] Compare SuYang/He Xin, Street as a Courtroom: State Accommodation of Labor Protests in South China, 44 Law & Society Review (March 2010), pp. 157–184 (178).

[36] Compare Zhang Haizheng, The Chinese bankruptcy law reforms in the past 10 years: perspectives and problems, 28 Journal of International Banking Law and Regulation (2013), pp. 395–402 (400).

this regard. More importantly, one also has to consider the constraints which the rule of law imposes on its addressees, including government authorities. The Chinese government has in fact occasionally ignored these constraints and taken action in order to be able to respond quickly and effectively to unwelcome developments.[37] In these cases values and political considerations other than the rule of law were given priority. It must be acknowledged in this regard that the Chinese development model, which arguably places less importance on the rule of law, but which is seen as a role model by many developing countries, has been very successful at least in the past.[38]

The Significance of the Rule of Law for China's Outbound Investments

The previous sections have highlighted the development of China's outbound investment activities in recent years as well as the status of the rule of law in general and in particular in China. This section now combines these two themes by asking if rule of law compliance is a success factor for China's outbound investment activities.

In the context of Chinese outbound investments, legal aspects and thus potentially also the rule of law are of multidimensional significance. They are related to law making, the implementation of legal rules and—from the viewpoint of the addressees of such rules—compliance or non-compliance. Furthermore, they also concern different legal regimes, namely China's own outbound investment system, the legal regimes of the target countries of China's outbound investments and—at the public international law level—treaty arrangements such as investment-related multilateral treaties, bilateral double taxation treaties, bilateral and multilateral investment treaties as well as other arrangements, including cooperation agreements concluded as part of the Belt and Road initiative.[39]

[37] Wolff (2016), *supra* note 27, pp. 608–609; Björn Ahl, Staatliche Eingriffe in den chinesischen Immobilienmarkt—Fragen der Rechtmässigkeit und des Rechtsschutzes (State Interventions in the Chinese Real Estate Market—Questions of Legality and Legal Protection), 45 Verfassung und Recht in Übersee (Constitution and Law Overseas) (2012), pp. 412–431, discussing the Beijing municipal government's reaction to the drastic increase in housing prices, which was effective but not in line with existing Chinese law.

[38] Ahl, ibid., p. 412; compare Georg Blume, *supra* note 11, pointing out that China has been able to free over one billion Chinese from bitter poverty.

[39] Wolff (2016), *supra* note 12, pp. 14–19.

Last but not least the rule of law also demands respect for agreements reached at the private law level, that is, for contracts concluded between Chinese outbound investors and their overseas partners, including not only private enterprises, but also government authorities.

Adherence to the rule of law means that China's outbound investment legal regime meets the requirements (at least) of the thin rule of law doctrine[40] and that the law governing outbound investments is applied as it is set.[41] The rule of law also implies that China respects its international treaty commitments. Furthermore, Chinese outbound investors have to comply with laws and regulations enacted at different levels in China and abroad governing their outbound investment activities.

It is rather obvious that disrespect for the rule of law carries certain risks for China's outbound investment strategies in general and for specific outbound investment projects in particular. First, the violation of existing legal obligations can of course result in liability and lead to legal proceedings and, ultimately, to awards, which may be enforceable against Chinese parties. Second, probably even more important is the reputational risk potentially arising out of the breach of existing obligations for China as such, for the Chinese government and particular government agencies as well as for Chinese multinational enterprises engaged in outbound investment activities. Chinese outbound investors, potential target countries and foreign business partners will take rule of law deficits into consideration when assessing the viability of any outbound investment project.

But does this mean that acceptance of the (Western) rule of law doctrine in general and specific legal commitments in particular is a crucial success factor for Chinese outbound investments? Is compliance with the rule of law really *conditio sine qua* non for Chinese outbound investments? One may doubt this in light of the fact that China has in the past often prioritized other goals and values over the rule of law. Take the above-quoted example of 2015 when the outbound remittance of funds was suddenly blocked in China for a period of about six months, thus bringing Chinese outbound investments to a complete stop.[42] This action was not supported by any legal basis,[43] but must rather be regarded as yet another

[40] *Supra*, Sect. 3.

[41] Wolff (2016), *supra* note 27, pp. 597–590.

[42] *Supra*, Sect. 2.

[43] Compare Latham & Watkins, *supra* note 8, p. 1.

example of the Chinese government's pragmatic approach when it comes to addressing problems in a hands-on manner.

Furthermore, at the public international law level in the famous South China Sea case,[44] the Republic of the Philippines had initiated arbitration proceedings against China according to Annex VII of the United Nations Convention of the Sea. The tribunal ruled that certain maritime claims made by China are not justified. China had declared that it would not recognize the tribunal, refused to participate in the arbitration proceedings and did not acknowledge the award.[45] Instead, China engaged in a checkbook diplomacy with the Philippines, which has subsequently not taken any further action based on the award rendered.[46]

Finally, in 2010–2011, Chinese firms had to face a "credibility and credit crisis" after the US securities regulator revoked the registrations of a large number of Chinese firms listed in the US due to suspected accounting irregularities.[47]

It would of course neither be fair nor justifiable to generalize these examples and to conclude that the rule of law does not play any role in China's outbound investments at all. However, it is important that the

[44] Compare Permanent Court of Arbitration, at https://pca-cpa.org/wp-content/uploads/sites/175/2016/07/PH-CN-20160712-Press-Release-No-11-English.pdf.

[45] Compare Jerome A. Cohen/Peter A. Dutton, Move Mountains, SCMP 22 July 2017, p. A 12: "Beijing has a lot of work to do to repair its international image. … What do other members of the UN sea convention think about China's blatant rejection of its commitment to the agreement's mandatory dispute settlement provisions?"

[46] Compare Mark J. Valencia, Amid China-US rivalry, Asean finds a role model in Duterte's Philippines, SCMP (2 April 2018), at http://www.scmp.com/comment/insight-opinion/article/2139937/amid-china-us-rivalry-asean-finds-role-model-dutertes; Alexis Romero, 9 China firms eye $9.5-billion new investments in Philippines, Philstar Global 11 April 2018, at https://www.philstar.com/headlines/2018/04/11/1804803/9-china-firms-eye-95-billion-new-investments-philippines.

[47] Wang He, Restoring confidence: Strengthening the regulatory system for PRC firms listing overseas, China Law & Practice (November 2011), at http://www.chinalawandpractice.com/sites/clp/2011/11/08/restoring-confidence-strengthening-the-regulatory-system-for-prc-firms-listing-overseas/?slreturn=20180319035400; also see T.J. Wong, Corporate Governance Research on Listed Companies in China: Institutions, Governance and Accountability, 9 Foundations and Trends in Accounting (No. 4) (2014), pp. 259–326 (314–318: "Challenges in applying Anglo-American accounting standards to a relationship-based governance system"); for the perceived influence of the Chinese Communist Party on China's multinational enterprises, see Richard McGregor, The Party (London: Penguin Books, 2011), pp. 34–69.

rule of law enjoys a very different status in China as compared with the West. Furthermore, one has to be realistic: its newly gained political and economic power may allow China to mitigate or even ignore rule of law concerns.[48] And the quoted examples seem to show that China is well aware of its own status.

Final Remark

Since the global financial crisis of 2008–2009 China has been expanding its global influence rapidly. In fact, China is now a global mega-power which pursues its own goals with full power, thus challenging the position(s) of the Western world. It remains to be seen if the West is strong enough to withstand and to which extent it is possible to uphold Western value systems, including the rule of law. Vice versa, China has to assess with great care if any disrespect for the rule of law can play out in its favor in the long run.

[48] Compare Sourabh Gupta, Look Closely—Trump has zero legal ammunition, SCMP—This Week in Asia 8–14 April 2018, p. 9.

CHAPTER 12

Sino-German Business Relations in Times of Structural Change: Working Toward More Reciprocity

Jürgen M. Geißinger and Britta Vasters

Foreign Investments: Characteristics of the US, EU and Germany

Chinese overseas investment in the European Union (EU) has been steadily increasing in recent years, with Germany being one of the major destinations for mergers and acquisitions. Germany's strong industrial manufacturing, computer hardware and automotive industries offer attractive investment opportunities for Chinese companies seeking growth and know-how. Washington's isolationist policies have significantly stunted the takeover ambitions of Chinese companies in the US domestic market. The transaction value of Chinese acquisitions in the US fell drastically in 2017 to about $10 billion, compared with a record of more than $50 billion in 2016.

J. M. Geißinger
MTU Aero Engines AG, Munich, Germany

B. Vasters (✉)
Economic Council – Wirtschaftsrat der CDU e. V., Berlin, Germany
e-mail: b.vasters@wirtschaftsrat.de

T. Wenniges, W. Lohman (eds.), *Chinese FDI in the EU and the US*,
https://doi.org/10.1007/978-981-13-6071-8_12

In comparison with the US or other European countries, Germany has by far the highest number of regulatory hurdles for investors. This includes but is not limited to building permission, environmental regulation and labor rights. However, the investment regulations in China depend on the business sector and the technology. Taken as a whole, China has clear rules and low regulations for the formation of a foreign company or business. If the business is defined as one of the "restricted industries", a foreign company in China is most likely forced to partner into a joint venture when entering the market.

After all, a joint venture must not necessarily be considered as negative. Besides easier market access it can also provide you with a broad range of essential network ("guanxi"). Furthermore, China recently has opened up one of its biggest industries to foreign ownership: BMW stands to become the first foreign car manufacturer to own a majority stake in a Chinese joint venture, showing Beijing is following through on a pledge to increasingly open up the economy to global corporations.

In terms of company acquisitions, the Chinese market is rather restrictive as a result of a nontransparent environment. At this juncture, it would be preferable to have equal requirements. China's government is aware that the current investment barriers not only stoke foreign discontent but are ultimately also detrimental to China's own economic welfare. Beijing has pledged to level the playing field for foreign investors and has made some initial progress in removing investment barriers. Thus, it is the task of the political leaders of the EU and China to work toward reciprocity in investment relations. The reciprocity principle is moreover the central norm of the General Agreement on Tariffs and Trade (GATT) and the World Trade Organization (WTO). A robust bilateral investment agreement with China should be the EU's priority.

Transparency is a crucial factor for investment decisions. In order to provide clear rules for Chinese investors in the European market, the current action plan of the European Commission is to be welcomed: On 13 September 2017, the European Commission announced the proposal for a regulation establishing a framework for screening of foreign direct investments (FDIs) into the EU ("draft regulation"). The draft regulation responds to reform considerations initially submitted by the Ministers for Economic Affairs of Germany, France and Italy to the Commission in February 2017. The reform is expected to come into force no earlier than 2019. Hence, foreign investors will have a more coherent picture of permissions, particular limitations or prohibitions.

There is reason to hope that the European Commission will create a more transparent framework than, for instance, the Committee on Foreign Investment in the United States (CFIUS) did. Especially the growing impact of the CFIUS is currently deterring potential foreign investors in the US. According to Baker McKenzie, in the first half of 2018, eight noteworthy deals have been canceled due to regulatory and political concerns, seven of them due to unresolved conflicts with CFIUS.

Recipe of Success: Trust—Definition—Vision

The most crucial requirement in order to succeed with your business in China is *trust*. It is indispensable to build trust not only with the business partners but also with the entire board of stakeholders. Personal relationships on all levels of hierarchy are the key to success and therefore should not be changed frequently.

Furthermore, it is necessary to have a clear *definition* of the business: If the business case is not based on a wholly foreign owned company, all rules of the cooperation and joint venture have to be defined. Once the agreement is reached, both sides have a detailed *vision* of the business, know the key indicators of success and are on equal terms of each other's expectations. Chinese are tough negotiation partners, but once a deal is agreed on and signed, they are not only very reliable partners, but also abide by the terms of contract.

Challenges on the Way

The fluctuation of local employees in China is often more than 10 percent and thus can be a challenge. Companies strongly compete with each other in order to attract specialized workers. German entrepreneurs with their own education center have to be aware of the fact that among 800 trainees or apprentices, only 300–400 will actually stay at the company. Almost half of the trained workers will be headhunted by other companies after having successfully undergone the well-proven German vocational training.

Everybody needs to have in mind that China is not a low-cost country and seeking for low-cost workers should not be the driver of the investment decision in China. China's per capita gross domestic product (GDP) was about $8000 in 2015, and is currently on track to break the $10,000 mark by 2020. Barring unexpected disruptions, China will have developed into a medium-to-high income country by around 2022. Hence, the driver of the investment decision is rather China's market opportunities and the good educated resources from the numerous Chinese universities.

In order to avoid infringing intellectual property (IP) rights, it is highly recommended to apply for patents in advance and technology must be well secured. For this reason, even patent families have to be applied—not only in China, but also globally. Due to the fact that the applications of patents are only in Chinese language, German companies have to be well prepared for a patent research. Over the past years, the meaning of patents has naturally risen in China, since leading Chinese companies have started to face infringing IP rights on their own.

Regarding the area or city of a future company location in China, again for "restricted industries", there is no or very limited freedom of choice for foreign entrepreneurs. Although this setting might seem one-sided beneficial or even obstructive at first glance, there are several advantages. The Chinese side will provide you with a good offer in return such as favorable estate, access to universities or workers and so on, aiming to achieve a win-win situation.

The upcoming regulation with the intention to increase and improve cyber security is becoming a challenge for all foreign companies in China. It is considered and planned that all company data have to be stored and operated on domestic Chinese servers. Foreign companies are anxious about the threat that sensitive data and information cannot be kept secret in future. However, the Data Protection Act has still not been fully elaborated and implemented, so the future development of data security must be kept very strictly in mind for fast and appropriate adjustments.

Benefits of Doing Business in China

Besides the market access and the tremendous number of potential customers, the Chinese market has great potential for German companies. The figures speak for themselves: In 2017, China's total spending on research and development is estimated to have hit 1.76 trillion yuan ($279 billion), a year-on-year increase of 14 percent. By using the local know-how and infrastructure, German companies will benefit from innovation not only *in* the market but also *for* the market.

China's Five-Year Plans are an integrated and all-embracing concept that is consistently built on one another. This contributes not only to a strong stability but also to security for investments—in clear contrast with, for example, Germany's sudden retreat from atomic power and the turnaround in energy policy.

During the 13th Five-Year Plan period, China's economy will move toward a "new normal", following an increasingly clear evolution toward a more sophisticated, better structured and more specialized mode of production. This new phase of and approach to development also create new space for sectoral growth, and new opportunities for inbound and outbound direct investment. China's traditional monopolies, state-run utilities and public services are gradually becoming accessible to private and even foreign investment.

This opens new channels for FDI into China and provides Chinese outbound investors with the opportunity to form valuable synergies and linkages between their domestic and overseas businesses. While China will enter a phase of medium-to-high growth over the next years, it will continue to be a main driver of global growth and generate enormous investment opportunities for businesses from around the world.

China's development has shifted gears in recent years. Emerging sectors such as services and high technology have taken the lead as the primary engines of growth, consumption has become the primary driver of growth and outbound investment has become the primary vehicle for growth. China has been gradually transforming to become an economic model defined by services, emerging industry, consumption and capital export, illustrating a national shift toward the middle-to-high end of the value chain. Over the course of this process, however, China must overcome challenges related to its relatively outdated technology, traditional business models and lack of experience investing overseas. This creates many opportunities for collaboration between Chinese and foreign companies.

On the one hand, Chinese companies can "go out" to acquire technology and business models for reintroduction into the domestic market, thereby pushing China to the middle-to-high end of the value chain. On the other hand, foreign investors can leverage their production technologies, business models and operational experience to accelerate the pace of China's transformation, providing important support for the economy's move toward the middle-to-high end. Chinese and foreign companies may find many mutually beneficial partnerships over the course of this process and will contribute significant impetus to the economy's push toward the middle-to-high end of the value chain.

Especially the following sectors may benefit from the development plan during the next years: information technology, biotechnology, agricultural technology and equipment, high-end manufacturing, environmentally friendly industries, new-energy technology, retail, education, healthcare and elderly care.

German companies are highly recommended to hire more employees with profound knowledge of the Chinese market and the Chinese language in order to create sustainable investment and long-term relations.

Economic Outlook

As relations with the US become increasingly difficult, the other economic giant, China, will inevitably become even more important to Germany. Furthermore, foreign investments in China also lead to a solid foundation of further expansion into the emerging markets of the Association of Southeast Asian Nations (ASEAN).

Against the backdrop of a rising transatlantic trade war and the limitation of the European market, German companies, particularly medium-sized businesses, must necessarily deal with the characteristics and dynamics of the Chinese market as well as with the international competition. Recapitulating, investments in China will have strong dynamics in the future and will therefore provide even further opportunities for German companies.

Printed by Printforce, the Netherlands